Academic Communication Skills

Conversation Strategies for
International Graduate Students

Li-Shih Huang

University Press of America,® Inc.
Lanham · Boulder · New York · Toronto · Plymouth, UK

Copyright © 2010 by
University Press of America,® Inc.
4501 Forbes Boulevard
Suite 200
Lanham, Maryland 20706
UPA Acquisitions Department (301) 459-3366

Estover Road
Plymouth PL6 7PY
United Kingdom

Library of Congress Control Number: 2010933276
ISBN: 978-0-7618-5280-3 (paperback : alk. paper)
eISBN: 978-0-7618-5281-0

TABLE OF CONTENTS

NOTES ON THE UNITS **99**

REFERENCES AND FURTHER READING **107**

SUBJECT INDEX **115**

ABOUT THE AUTHOR **117**

ACKNOWLEDGEMENTS

Grateful acknowledgement is given to the following publishers, journals, and authors for permission to reprint or adapt previously published materials.

Waveland Press, Inc. for "Exercise 1: Practicing vocabulary strategies" by Smith, J., Meyers, C. M., & Burkhalter, A. M. from *Communicate: Strategies for international teaching assistants*, pp. 149-150, copyright © 1992 (reissued 2007), with permission from Waveland Press, Inc.

Sage Publications for the article reprinted from "Fine-tuning the craft of teaching by discussion" by L.-S. Huang, from *Business Communication Quarterly*, Vol. 68(4), pp. 492-500, copyright © 2005, with permission from Sage Publications.

Taylor and Francis Ltd. for the article reprinted from "Practicing speaking for academic purposes using Aristotle's *Topics*" by L.-S. Huang, from *Communication Teacher*, Vol. 21, pp. 62-67, copyright © 2007 National Communication Association, with permission from Taylor and Francis Ltd. (http://www.tandf.co.uk/journals) on behalf of The National Communication Association.

TESOL, Inc. for the article reprinted from "ESL for academic purposes: Pathway to participating in academic discussion through informal debate" by L.-S. Huang, from *TESOL Journal*, Vol. 11(4), pp. 30-31, copyright © 2002, with permission from Copyright.

I am indebted to those who have helped, directly or indirectly, with the publication of this book.

UNIT 1

GETTING STARTED: A GUIDE TO KEY TERMS AND CONCEPTS

1.1 Unit Introduction

Unit 1 introduces the key terms that you will need to understand as you embark on the activities presented in this book. The purpose is not to comprehensively review commonly used terms and concepts in such fields as Applied Linguistics, Second Language Pedagogy, and Anthropology, but to increase your familiarity with the concepts so that you can self-diagnose your speaking choices and challenges in academic settings.

Culturally shaped preferences can cause many types of miscommunication, and thus throughout the book, you will be asked to return to the preferences introduced in this unit to explore the challenges that might arise in a range of academic situations. Through self-analysis, you will evaluate what you need to consider and then prepare yourself to practice and monitor your speaking when experimenting with the application activities suggested in the book and when engaging in daily speaking encounters. The aim is to promote transferability through a recursive cycle of learning that involves both socially interactive and self-reflective activities.

1.2   A Little Bit of Theory: Key Terms and Concepts

Cultural values vary considerably. A culture is a shared system of symbols, beliefs, attitudes, values, expectations, and norms for behaviour. Members of a culture may share similar assumptions about how people should think, behave, and communicate. Researchers (e.g., Ulijn & Campbell, 1999; Ulijn & Kumar, 1999) propose an iceberg metaphor to explain the complexity of any culture. The iceberg includes an explicit, visible layer, which represents facts, and a much larger, implicit, invisible layer, which represents unconscious rules or hidden assumptions. When speaking with someone from another culture, you might encode messages based on your own assumptions, which reside in the implicit layer of your own culture, whereas your listener may decode your messages according to assumptions that reside in the implicit layer of his/her culture.

Many international students come from educational environments that differ from those in North America. Differences in academic traditions mean that many students have very different expectations about how learners are supposed to behave, and also about how teachers should behave. Where two sets of expectations intersect, linguistic and paralinguistic cues can have vastly different meanings; these differences may create varied responses when people use them in cross-cultural contexts, and opportunities for misunderstandings and miscommunications may arise.

The following factors will help you better understand the range of predictable, particular academic situations covered in this book.

High/low context

One way to understand intercultural communication (i.e., communication that occurs in encounters between people from different cultural backgrounds) (Scollon & Scollon, 2001; Spencer-Oatey, 2000) is to consider the cultural preferences for certain communication patterns that various researchers have examined in their efforts to link cultural norms to communication and linguistic patterns. Anthropologist Edward T. Hall (1976) distinguishes between low-context and high-context cultures to describe cultural differences in communication patterns. Context is related to whether what is being communicated is inherent in the setting and is already understood by the speakers involved (i.e., high context) or whether speakers must communicate most of the information overtly through the spoken exchange of messages (i.e., low context). According to Hall, individuals from low-context cultures, including those in North America, German-speaking countries, and Scandinavian countries, tend to be verbally explicit and do not rely on a store of shared assumptions and implicit information that are present in the context of an event; these individuals may prefer to use a direct and linear discourse in communication and to provide contextual information, such as facts, figures, statistics, and other pieces of background information, to their listeners.

In high-context cultures, like those in Japan, China, and Arab and Latin American countries, most information is either contained in the physical context of an event or internalized in the interlocutors, and thus when communicating, individuals rely more on shared knowledge and assumptions. This reliance may manifest in indirect, circular communication patterns. High-context cultural speakers tend to be more verbally implicit; they often rely more on nonverbal cues and use more indirect, subtle, and circular communication patterns.Without over generalizing, the suggestion can be made, for example, that a speaker's tendency to communicate in a high-context manner may lead him/her to knowingly (to avoid insulting the other speaker's knowledge) or unknowingly (through habitual, preferred communication patterns that have reached automaticity) overlook the important contextual clues needed to clarify meanings during communication. An example that typifies the situations that I have encountered in my years of teaching is the case of one of my students who was pursuing a doctoral degree in medical sciences. This student had worked at a major hospital in Canada for over five years and told me that he needed to improve his pronunciation and vocabulary because of the communication challenges that he had with his colleagues. After analyzing one of his dialogical exchanges, he had an "a-ha" moment when he realized that his perceived inability to communicate with his colleagues had very little, if anything at all, to do with a lack of vocabulary or competence in using precise words and terms in his communication or his "non-native" accent. Instead, the difficulties resulted from his preference for inductive reasoning, which is one of the key characteristics of high-context cultures, and for an indirect and circular communication style. From his colleagues' perspective, his digressions or the need to establish all his reasons or evidence before stating his request or main point made him take too long to get to the point, which led to communication breakdowns. He, in turn, was often perplexed about his North American colleagues' directness and explicitness, which he interpreted as insulting and unfriendly at times (Huang, 2009/2010).

It's important to guard against assuming that people from a specific contextual cultural orientation tend to ~~~~~icate in a certain way at all times, however. Within a particular culture, the degree of explicitness or implicitness, or tion needs to be explicitly transmitted or coded in a message, may vary, depending on such factors as ir, audience, purpose, and so on. For example, the interactions of two people from a low-context culture know each other very well, such as two very good friends or two people who specialize in a particular form of high-context communication.

Large/small power distance

The power distance preference – how cultures distribute power, rank, and status among members – is a key factor that deals with the issue of human inequality. This preference may influence how people interact and communicate with each other. Using concepts originally developed by the social psychologist Mulder, who analyses interpersonal power dynamics, Hofstede's study suggests that power distance is a characteristic of cultures and defines it as "the extent to which less powerful members of institutions and organizations within a country expect and accept that power is distributed unequally" (1997, p. 28). According to Hofstede, power distances are "to a considerable extent societally determined" (2001, p. 79).

While people from some cultures may value equality or strive for equal status (i.e., small power distance), other cultures accept and expect that power is distributed unequally or even greatly value status differentials and social hierarchies (i.e., large power distance). In the latter cases, people tend not to communicate with those of higher status directly, and tend to accept the words and actions of individuals with higher status without question, debate, or criticism. Your view of power and status differentials may influence how you behave or communicate, or how you expect others of different rankings or statuses to behave in various communicative settings. For instance, how do you feel about asking questions in class? How likely are you to disagree with a professor during a discussion, when you are certain that your professor needs to be corrected? Would you openly disagree with your instructor in a seminar discussion or challenge an expert's viewpoint at a colloquium? How comfortable is it for you to address your instructor by his/her first name? How comfortable do you feel about dropping by your professor's office just to say "hello," and how often do you do it? How do you feel about questioning or criticizing authorities? Your responses to these questions may indicate how you perceive power distance and how such an important factor comes into play in your interactions with others.

The implications of the degree of power distance that a culture prefers are evident in the relationships between students and instructors. In various speaking situations, speakers who value large power differences (e.g., in the Philippines, Mexico, Venezuela, India, and Singapore) are likely to show respect for authority, use formal language that emphasizes distinctions based on a social hierarchy and that is filled with power/hierarchy indicators, be silent or listen quietly as a form of respect, not take initiatives out of respect for superiors or the belief that the subordinate should be told what to do, be reluctant to disagree or criticize authority, show respect by agreeing politely, be hesitant about asking questions because they might pose a threat to the teacher's authority, avoid confrontations, and expect that instructors or presenters should have answers to all questions. People from small power-distance cultures (e.g., Austria, Israel, Denmark, New Zealand, the United States, and Canada), in contrast, tend to consider it their right to question the instructor or the speaker and express their personal opinions. Educational systems in those countries may also reinforce small power distance values by teaching students to ask critical questions and to challenge arguments (e.g., Lustig & Koester, 1993; Hofstede, 1984).

Individualism and collectivism

This dimension relates to "the relationship between the individual and the collectivity that prevails in a given society" (Hofstede, 2001, p. 209). According to Hofstede, in collectivist cultures, people are interdependent within their in-groups (family, tribe, nation, etc.), give priority to the goals of their in-groups, and shape their behaviour primarily on the basis of in-group norms. In contrast, in individualist cultures, people tend to see themselves as autonomous and independent from their in-groups; they give priority to their personal goals over their in-group's goals. They also behave primarily on the basis of their own attitudes rather than on the norms of their in-groups. The differences between the two cultural orientations may include these characteristics: individualistic societies emphasize "I" consciousness, autonomy, independence, and individual initiative; collectivist societies, in contrast, stress "we" consciousness, collective identity, group harmony, group decisions, and so on.

Key differences between individualist and collectivist societies that may manifest in school settings include the following: In cultures with an individualist orientation, identity is based on the individual person, whereas for the collectivist, it is group identity. In people's approaches to task completion, for the individualist, the importance of accomplishing the task tends to take precedence over relationship building in group work situations, whereas for those of the collectivist orientation, relationship building tends to precede task completion. In addition, in individualist cultures, generally, people should strive to maintain harmony and avoid conflict. When participating in class discussions, students with a collectivist orientation tend to be more reluctant to speak up in class or in large groups, whereas in individualist cultures, speaking one's mind or expressing one's opinion is valued. Individual initiatives are discouraged in collectivist societies, whereas such initiatives are often encouraged and viewed favourably in individualist societies. Some cultures (e.g., in North America, Australia, Great Britain, Netherlands, and New Zealand) tend to accept, encourage, or reward individualism; others (e.g., in Central and South America, Taiwan, South Korea, Vietnam, Thailand, and China) tend to frown on behaviours that reflect individualism and instead stress the value of collective behaviours.

It's important to note also that, although these dimensions of culture represent the patterns of most people in a given culture, individuals differ in the amount of individualism and collectivism they represent and accept for themselves. Furthermore, no society can be either exclusively individualistic or collective in orientation.

Masculinity and femininity

According to Hofstede (2001), the dimension of masculinity and femininity deals with what implications the biological differences between the sexes should have for their respective social roles (p. 279). He labels those who strive for maximal distinction between what women and men are expected to do as "masculine" cultures (e.g., Japan, Austria, Venezuela, and Mexico). Those labelled as "feminine" cultures (e.g., Sweden, Norway, the Netherlands, and Denmark) permit more overlapping social roles for the two genders.

Members of highly masculine cultures (e.g., Slovakia, Japan, Austria, Venezuela, and Italy) tend to believe that men should be assertive and that women should be nurturing. Gender roles are clearly differentiated, and gender inequality is accepted as the norm. The reverse is true for members of highly feminine cultures (e.g., Sweden, Norway, Netherlands, and Denmark): Gender roles are less rigid and equality between the genders is the norm. The United States and Canada have been identified as countries with masculine cultures (e.g., Nelson, Brunel, Supphellen, & Manchanda, 2006). This categorization indicates a higher degree of gender role differentiation.

Gender differences and values have been extensively examined and discussed by Deborah Tannen (1992), who has shown the difference between female and male discourses in the United States. Her work has shown that each gender has its own way of thinking, feeling, speaking, and behaving. Men and women can be very different in their patterns of communication. It is important not to use this information to stereotype gender differences. Instead, use the information to increase your awareness of whether or how gender differences may be a factor in styles of both verbal and non-verbal communication in order to avoid miscommunication and to work together more effectively.

Tolerance for ambiguity/uncertainty avoidance

Uncertainty avoidance as a cultural characteristic deals with how people from different cultures handle unexpected, potentially confusing situations. Cultures differ in the extent to which people prefer and can tolerate ambiguity, and therefore individuals tend to select different mediational means for coping with situations that they perceive as unstructured, unclear, or unpredictable. According to Hofstede's research (1984), at one extreme are cultures such as those of Denmark, Jamaica, Ireland, the United States, and Canada, all of which have relatively low uncertainty avoidance. These cultures therefore have a high tolerance for uncertainty and ambiguity. Conversely, the cultures of Greece, Guatemala, Portugal, and Uruguay all have relatively high uncertainty avoidance. These cultures therefore prefer to ensure certainty through demanding rules and regulations that constrain human behaviours.

Differences in the preferred level of uncertainty avoidance can lead to problems in communication. For example, a student with high uncertainty avoidance, who feels most comfortable with clear structures, rules, and parameters and less comfortable with ambiguity and unpredictability, tends to prefer explicit instructions and knowing the "correct" answers. Such a student therefore might become frustrated by a direction to "choose your own topic" or by the autonomous learning approach preferred by a professor who exhibits a low uncertainty avoidance style of communicating.

Silence

The role of silence in communication has received growing attention in recent years, and researchers recognize that silence is not simply an absence of speech, but instead has forms (e.g., some individuals remain silent while others engage in discussion) and functions (i.e., cognitive for processing language, discursive for marking discourse boundaries, social for politeness strategies, for example, and affective for managing emotions) that constitute an important part of communication and the perceived amount of silence can be a source of stereotyping (see Nakane, 2005, 2007). The fact that silence is more unconscious than speech makes it challenging to learn how to use it. As Saville-Troike (1985) pointed out:

> Learning appropriate rules for silence is also part of the acculturation process for adults attempting to develop communicative competence in a second language and culture. Perhaps because it funds at a lower level of consciousness than speech, many (perhaps most) otherwise fluent bilinguals retain a foreign "accent" in their use of silence in the second language, retaining native silence patterns even as they use the new verbal structures. (pp. 12-13)

Many have argued that culture-specific uses of silence convey information about cultural norms and attitudes about talking vs. silence (e.g., Kim, 2002; Saville-Troike, 1984). Silence may involve inter-turn (between interlocutors) and intra-turn (within the same speaker) pauses, non-participation in conversation, or lack of speech in interactive situations, and the value of silence in communication varies greatly from one culture to the next. Stereotyping and misunderstanding may occur when the characteristic use of silence by members of one speech community is interpreted according to the norms and rules accepted by members of another speech community.

In terms of attitudes toward silence, researchers suggest that Western cultures prefer talk to silence, whereas, in contrast, more positive values may be attached to silence in the East (Giles et al., 1991; Scollon & Scollon, 1995). Some cultures have tended to celebrate excellent verbal performance as a vehicle for self-expression and a measure of success; in these cultures, there tends to be an aversion to silence, in the sense that people find it awkward or embarrassing. Silence in class or in an academic seminar may be misinterpreted as lack of interest, an unwillingness to communicate, shyness, or a lack of oral proficiency or communication skills. One example of how the factor of silence comes into play in communication is the case of a Ph.D. candidate, who, during his thesis defense, took excessively long pauses to compose his thoughts and responses after each question, without giving any eye contact or any verbal or nonverbal signals to indicate that he was thinking. His communication style, which might have been interpreted as deliberate, careful thinking on an important occasion, instead was perceived as a lack of knowledge, which ultimately led to an unsuccessful thesis defense.

One must be cautious, however, about stereotypes surrounding silence and talk and about the comparisons often made between "Western" and "non-Western" cultures. It is important to be aware of possible situational, contextual, individual, intranational, or intraregional variations, rather than over simplistically attributing silence to a particular ethnic or national background.

Proxemics

Proxemics involves an individual's perception and use of space within a cultural context. Hall, who developed this field, defines "the study of [a human's] transactions as [he/she] perceives and uses intimate, personal, social and public space in various settings while following out-of-awareness dictates of cultural paradigms" (1974, p. 2). Hall's definition has three key components. First, proxemics involves the study of transactions in interpersonal interactions. Second, these interactions are viewed in a spatial context, which Hall defines as intimate, personal, social, and public zones. Third, the behaviours associated with these interactions are considered to be largely learned or culturally determined rather than entirely dictated by innate biological or physiological processes. Hall argues that human perceptions and use of space, although derived from a sensory apparatus that all humans share, are molded and patterned by culture and convey meanings. People internalize the cultural rules of proxemics at an unconscious level, and violating such rules in communication can lead to misunderstanding or communication breakdowns in cross-cultural settings.

People have certain patterns for delimiting distance when they interact, and this distance varies according to the nature of the social interaction. Hall (1966) suggests that people interact within four spatial zones or distances: *intimate, personal, social,* and *public.* These proxemic zones are characterized by differences in the ways that people relate to one another and in the behaviours that typify the communication that will probably occur in them. For Americans, Hall's observations suggest that intimate space ranges from 0 to 18 inches and is the closest "bubble" of space surrounding a person. Intimate space is the interaction distance for closest friends and intimates. Personal space, which ranges from 18 inches to 4 feet, includes a close phase that is within touching distance, and a far phase, i.e., "an arm's length." Social space, which is a distance ranging from 4 to 12 feet, also includes a close phase (i.e., 4 to 6 feet), which is the interaction distance for acquaintances or for informal interaction, and a far phase (i.e., 7 to 12 feet), which is the interaction distance for strangers or for more formal interaction. Public space is any distance over 12 feet and represents the distance beyond which people will perceive an interaction as impersonal and relatively anonymous, such as in a public speaking situation. Hall's observations show that, for example, those from warmer climates, e.g., Latin America, prefer close distances, whereas those from colder climates, e.g., Nordic cultures, seem to prefer relatively large physical distances during interpersonal communication.

Proxemics is one of the most important aspects of nonverbal communication. As Hall and Hall (1990) state:

Since most people don't think about personal distance as something that is culturally patterned, foreign spatial cues are almost inevitably misinterpreted. This can lead to bad feelings which are then projected onto the people from the other culture in a most personal way. When a foreigner appears aggressive and pushy, or remote and cold, it may mean only that her or his personal distance is different from yours.

It is essential to understand that the distance or space we feel we need is influenced by social norms, situational factors, the personality characteristics of those around us, as well as our own characteristics and the level of familiarity. One needs to become aware of one's own culture's proxemic patterns and the patterns of interlocutors by observing, for example, whether either speaker tries to move closer or further away in an attempt to maintain the appropriate conversational distance. Invasion of personal space during communication may be disruptive in an encounter and may undermine comprehension, lead to communication apprehension, and be the source of negative interpersonal perceptions or evaluations (e.g., Buller, 1987/2005). All this may occur even when the speaker is not aware of the issue. As with learning about and using silence discussed earlier, understanding proxemics in intercultural communication can help you avoid misunderstandings or misperceptions.

Time

Chronemics is the study of time usage in nonverbal communication. Cultures differ in the ways people perceive and react to time; misunderstandings can occur between people who perceive and use time differently. Differing perceptions can be expressed through punctuality, willingness to wait, speed of speech, or even the amount of time people are willing to listen. The timing and frequency of any action, as well as the tempo of speech within an interaction, contribute to the process of non-verbal communication.

"Time orientation" refers to the value or importance that members of a culture place on the passage of time. Past-oriented cultures, such as China's, regard previous experiences and events as most important, and, as such, people with this time orientation emphasize tradition and show much deference and respect for parents and other elders. In problem-solving *Academic Communication Skills: Conversational Strategies for International Graduate Students*

situations, tried and true methods may be applied. Present-oriented cultures, such as those in Central and South American countries, regard current experiences as the most valuable ones. People who have this orientation tend to emphasize immediacy. Future-oriented cultures, i.e., those of many European Americans, tend to view tomorrow as the most important. People with this orientation tend to look at the potential future benefits that might be obtained from one's actions. The natural tendency to view one's own preferred orientation as superior to those of others can be a source of problems in intercultural communication.

Attitudes toward time may include agreements among the members of a culture on such issues as the extent to which time is regarded as valuable commodity and the assumptions that members of cultures make about how time should be experienced. In a "monochromic time system," people are expected to do one thing at a time and time is segmented into precise, small units; in a "polychromic time system," in contrast, people generally do several things at the same time. In polychromic cultures, such as those of Central and South America, relationships tend to precede schedules. Misinterpretations can occur when individuals from monochromic and polychromic cultures attempt to interact, because individuals may view another person's response to time as disrespectful (a perception of a person from a monochromic culture) or unfriendly (a perception of a person from a polychromic culture). This factor may also come into play in approaches to task completion, for example, where participants from different cultural time systems need to be aware of the time system that they tend to use to regulate their behaviours and also need to adapt to the time orientations of others.

Affective factors

In addition to considering cultural differences in relation to any of the above dimensions, one must not neglect the role that various affective factors, such as willingness to communicate, inhibition, impulsivity, and extroversion, play in communication. To touch on each briefly, willingness to communicate may be defined as "an underlying continuum representing the predisposition toward or away from communicating, given the choice" (MacIntyre et al., 2002, p. 538). Such a predisposition may be target-language related or may have its roots in one's first-language communication patterns. Furthermore, having a high level of communicative ability does not necessarily correspond to a high willingness to communicate (MacIntyre et al., 1998). Rather, one's willingness to communicate may be related to various factors, such as group climate, self-confidence, personalities, and motivation.

We can all identify with the fact that learning an additional language necessitates making mistakes and errors, but some may perceive mistakes and errors as threats to the ego. Apprehension or fear of showing self-doubt leads to the construction of mechanisms for protective self-defense and can inhibit one's willingness to participate or to take risks in speaking publicly. This leads us to the factor of being impulsive/intuitive versus reflective/systematic. Individuals with an impulsive/intuitive style tend to be more willing to venture a guess, whereas reflective/systematic individuals tend to weigh all considerations about an issue before venturing an answer.

Finally, extroversion is another potentially important factor in communication. An "extrovert" needs to receive ego enhancement from others, as opposed to deriving that affirmation within oneself, as in introversion (Brown, 2006). This factor is relevant in face-to-face interactions. As established in this unit, cross-cultural norms of verbal and nonverbal interaction may differ widely, and it is important to be aware that what may appear to be introversion in one culture may mean something else (e.g., politeness or respect) in another. In speaking situations across various academic contexts, one needs to be sensitive to an individual's attitudes about speaking out in a public setting and to cultural norms, as well as to individual preferences.

A final note

The cultural dimensions and individual factors covered in this unit are by no means comprehensive, and one should not overlook the complexity, situatedness, and interrelatedness of those factors or dimensions in communication. I encourage you to enhance awareness and understanding and to achieve mastery through further reading, discussions of the questions included in each unit, practical experimentation, and personal observation of your own and others' communication patterns. Learn from generalizations about other cultures, but do not use them to stereotype or oversimplify your ideas about another person or culture. Instead, use generalizations to help you understand and appreciate the diverse qualities of the people you meet. Remember that cultural norms may not apply to the behaviours of any particular individual. We are all shaped by many, many factors – our ethnic backgrounds, families, education, personalities – and are more complicated than any particular cultural norm would suggest. Check your interpretations when you are uncertain, and keep questioning your assumptions about the "right way" to communicate.

1.3   Facing Challenges and Exploring Hidden Assumptions

Diagnostic questions: Explore these questions on your own if you are using this book for self-study. In a classroom, share your thoughts about these questions with a speaking partner and be prepared to share your discussion with the class.

1.   How do you identify yourself in terms of your communication preferences, as presented in this unit?

2.   How do you think that these factors might influence your own actions as a student, research assistant, and/or teaching assistant, as well as your expectations of your instructors or supervising professors?

UNIT 2

ENGAGING IN INTERPERSONAL COMMUNICATION

2.1 Unit Introduction

The content covered in Units 2 through 7 is intended to help you meet identified challenges with specific strategies as you participate in increasingly larger and more complex conversational groups. Unit 2 focuses on interpersonal communication and is designed to help you enter, maintain, and exit conversations with ease and confidence. The diagnostic section includes questions that will help you explore potential communication challenges during initial interpersonal encounters. The mechanics of language needed to master interpersonal communication, such as face-to-face meetings, small talks, and telephone conversations, are introduced before four classroom-tested application activities designed to help you put the mechanics into practice. This unit concludes with strategies for leaving phone messages, making new acquaintances, maintaining conversations, and practicing active listening skills that aim to facilitate your continuing development and success.

2.2   Facing Challenges and Exploring Hidden Assumptions

Diagnostic questions: Explore these questions on your own if you are using this book for self-study. In a classroom, share your thoughts about these questions with a speaking partner and be prepared to share your discussion with the class.

1.   How would you address your professor (Dr., Professor, or by his/her first name)? How do you decide which form to use? What cultural factors might influence your choices or preferences in how you address others?

(Note 1)

2.   If you were sitting down and someone introduced you to a friend of his/hers, under what circumstances would you stand up?

3.   What gestures or expressions are used in your country when one meets someone new?

4.   What is small talk? Is small talk really small?

5.   When you talk to a person you have never met before, how do you know what topics are appropriate for you to discuss? In your culture, what kinds of things would you talk about to get acquainted with someone? Are there any topics that you would consider inappropriate to discuss with a new acquaintance? Are there any questions that you would not ask?

6.   Is it easier for you to speak English on the phone or face-to-face? Why? What problems have you had using English on the phone? What do you think has caused these problems? What strategies could you use to overcome them?

2.3 Mastering the Mechanics of Language

This section first covers mechanics and strategies for speaking on the telephone, which even advanced learners can find challenging because of the lack of paralinguistic cues in such conversations. Then the mechanics and strategies for entering, maintaining, and exiting conversations are introduced. This section concludes with functional language for making an appointment, seeking advice, and expressing gratitude. (For functional language for offering advice, refer to Unit 6, which focuses on conversation skills in the teaching context.)

(A) Telephone conversations Here are some common telephone English phrases that you might use in different conversational moves. Practice until they become automatic, so that you can focus on the content of the message that you are trying to convey or that you are receiving.

Introduction:

This is [name].

This is [name]calling.

This is [name]speaking.

My name is [name], from the department of....

(Note: If you are calling someone you don't know or someone you think might not recognize your name, provide a piece of additional information, as in "Hello. This is X, your classmate." "Hello. This is [name] calling from the department of....")

Try adding some of your own expressions:

_____

_____

Asking for someone:

Is this Dr. [name]'s office?

Is X there/home?

May I have extension 3665, please?

May I speak to..., please?

Could you put me through to...?

Try adding some of your own expressions:

_____

_____

Reason for calling:

I am calling to make an appointment with you to discuss my research project....

I am calling to find out more information about....

I am calling on behalf of (someone)....

This is X returning your call.

Try adding some of your own expressions:

_____

_____

Telling a caller that someone is not available:

I'm afraid (that)...is not available at the moment.

Dr. X is out at the moment.

I'm sorry, but Professor X is in a meeting now.

I'm sorry, but he/she is not in right now.

I'm sorry, but she's out for lunch right now.

I'm sorry, but Professor X won't be back (to the office) until....

Try adding some of your own expressions:

_____

_____

Asking who is on the phone:

Could I have your name, please?   Who is calling please?
May I ask/know who is calling, please?   To whom am I speaking?

Try adding some of your own expressions:

Connecting someone:

Could you please hold the line?   Hold on a minute/second, please.
Could you hold on for a second, please?   Would you mind holding?

Try adding some of your own expressions:

Thanking the caller for waiting:

Thanks for holding.   Sorry for the delay.

Try adding some of your own expressions:

Taking a message:

May I take a message?   Would you like to leave a message?
Could you speak more slowly, please?   Could I have your name and telephone number, please?
Could you spell your name, please?   Could you please repeat the number/your name?
I'll make sure that X gets this message (ASAP).   It's [name], and your phone number is [number]. Is that correct?

Try adding some of your own expressions:

Closing:

Thank you (very much) for your help.   Thanks for taking such a lengthy message.
Thanks (very much) for calling.   (It's) nice talking with you (again).
I'll send you an e-mail to confirm our meeting.   (Note 2)

Try adding some of your own expressions:

Others:

I'm sorry. You have the wrong number.   I'm afraid you've dialled the wrong number.
I'm sorry. There is no one here by that name.

Try adding some of your own expressions:

(B) Leaving a phone message

Have you found yourself reluctant to leave a phone message or inclined to hang up the phone when it's time to leave someone a voice mail? Follow this easy outline to ensure that the recipient of the message has all the information he/she needs.

1. Greetings and introduction:

Good Morning/Afternoon/Evening, this message is for X.
Hello, my name is X.

Hello, this is X calling.
Hi, this is X returning your call.

2. State the time of the day and your reason for calling:

It's 9:30 in the morning. I'm calling

to find out if....
to see if....
to let you know that....
to tell you that....

3. Make a request:

Could you please call me back when you have a moment?
Could you please give me a call when you get a chance?
Would you mind giving me a call when you get this message?
I'd appreciate it if you could please give me a call back sometime this afternoon.

4. Leave your name/telephone number:

My name is [name] and it's spelled x-x-x-x-x . My (phone/telephone) number is.... (Note: Repeat the number.)
You can reach me at....
Once again, this is [name] calling, and you can reach me at....
Please call me at [phone number] anytime after 3:00 p.m.

5. Closing:

Thank you. Bye.
I'll talk to you soon. Take care. Bye.

I look forward to talking to you soon.
I hope to hear from you soon.

(Note 3)

What other expressions do you use or have you heard others use? Try adding them to the list as you continue to expand your linguistic repertoire.

(C) Entering and maintaining conversations

Small talk may not be so small after all. If you feel some trepidation about what to say or how to initiate a conversation, you are not alone! Small talk is the social lubricant that facilitates connections and interactions with those whom you meet in the academic community. Consider the times when you happen to run into people on the street, in the hallway, at the cafeteria, at departmental social or academic gatherings, or at conferences. Those encounters present opportunities for you to enhance your ability to engage in small talk, and, most importantly, to build connections that can lead to professional conversations. Use those opportunities to convey genuine interest, warmth, and care for others and their activities. This kind of interaction will in turn encourage them to speak to you in future encounters.

Here are two-step small talk strategies adapted from J. Freeman's (2004) handouts ("The Mechanics of Small Talk") that you can apply to get you started on taking the first important steps to engaging in small talk in academic settings.

Step 1: Warm-up -- Greetings and responses

Useful greeting phrases:	**Useful responding phrases:**
How are you?	I'm well. How about you?
How have you been?	I'm doing well. Thanks.
It's nice to see you again.	Yes. How have you been?
I haven't seen you for a while.	Yes. I haven't seen you for ages! What's new?
How was your conference trip to Ottawa over reading break?	Great! Were you away too?
I see you are back from your trip. When did you get back?	Yesterday, and how are things with you?
How was your holiday?	Great! Did you have a nice holiday too?

What other expressions do you or your speaking partners use? As you experiment with familiar or unfamiliar expressions used to initiate a conversation, listen carefully to how others respond to your greetings and add the responses to your list.

Step 2: Topics to keep the conversation going

Even highly proficient learners of English are quick to share stories about their awkward silent moments when they did not know what to say after Step 1. Do you sometimes not know what to do after you have entered the conversation? If the time and occasion permit you to engage in a longer conversation, then seize the opportunity to get to know your interlocutor better. Your interactions will form the basis for future conversations. These social exchanges may make it easy to talk about other professional matters.

Try to think of common topics that you can use to keep the dialogue going, topics such as responses to your greetings, the weather, courses, TA work, research work, current events in the news, a previous contact or the last conversation, or the location where you both are. Here are some examples to get you started:

1. *Responses to your greetings:*

Response:	I am exhausted.	Why is that?
	Hectic! (In response to: How's your morning so far?)	What's a hectic morning like for you?

Try adding some of your own expressions:

2. *Weather:*   What a gorgeous day!   The weather has really turned out nice today!
                  It's a bit chilly today, isn't it?   Looks like we will have the same weather during the next few days!

Try adding some of your own expressions:

3. *Course work:* What courses are you taking this term?   Are you taking (e.g., course number) this term?
How many courses are you taking this term?
I'm taking Professor Saxon's course this term. Have you ever taken a course with her?
Have you finished the reading for Wednesday's class? What did you think of the piece?
How's your class presentation coming along? What did you decide to focus on?
I recently visited Professor Lutz's course website created by the students who are taking one of his courses. Have you ever visited that website?

Try adding some of your own expressions:

_____

_____

4. *TA work:*   What course are you TAing this term?   Are you TAing multiple courses this term?

Try adding some of your own expressions:

_____

_____

5. *Research:*   How is your research going?   What area of research are you working on?
How's your thesis/proposal coming along?   How's your data analysis coming along?
Have you finished the data collection for your research?
Are you applying for a research grant this year?
Are you planning to attend the TESOL conference this year?
Are you thinking about submitting a proposal for the upcoming conference in Boston?
Did you ever take the grant application workshop offered by the university? Was it helpful?
I hear that you collaborated with Dr. Kelly on her research project. What was the research project about?
I hear that you used to work at the University of Toronto. How did you like working there?

Try adding some of your own expressions:

_____

_____

6. *News:* Have you been following the news in Haiti?   Have you heard the news about…?

Try adding some of your own expressions:

_____

_____

7. *Previous contact:*   That was a great gathering we had at Leslie's, eh?
I don't know if you remember me, but I'm Michael. We met at….
How's Nicholas doing these days? I haven't seen him since our last gathering.
The last time I saw you, you were about to head off to a conference in New York. How was it?
If I remember correctly, you are planning to defend your thesis this month. How does that feel?
Did you manage to submit that manuscript last week, as you hoped?
The last time I saw you, you were going to see *Avatar*. Was it as visually amazing as it was said to be by everyone who saw it?

Try adding some of your own expressions:

_____

_____

8. *Location:* Do you live around here?   Do you have a class in this building?
        What brings you here today?   I didn't know that you are attending this conference too!

Try adding some of your own expressions:

_____

_____

9. *Personal:* Here are some useful phrases for showing that you are aware of the potential intrusiveness of asking a question in interpersonal communication.

    I was wondering if I could ask you.... Could I ask you...?
    Could you please tell me...?   Would you mind telling me...?
    I would be interested in knowing.... May I ask you...?
    You don't have to answer the question if you don't feel comfortable answering.

Try adding some of your own expressions:

_____

_____

10. *Other:* Last week I saw the documentary *The Lost Tomb of Jesus*. Have you seen it?
      On Friday, I went with some friends to see *Sherlock Homes*. Have you seen it?
      There was a really good article about language and thought in *The Globe and Mail* last week that might be
      of interest to you.
      I saw your name on the list for the steering committee meeting scheduled for next week. How long have
      you been serving on the committee?

Try adding some of your own expressions:

_____

_____

(Note4)

(D) Exiting Conversations

Have you ever run into a person and not known how to exit the brief conversation because both of you might be on your way somewhere? Have you ever found yourself in the middle of a conversation and then realized that you must head somewhere and so need to end the conversation? How do you exit a conversation politely? If you are in a hurry or can't talk for too long, then it is important that you let your interlocutor know; it's also important to respect the hints that others provide. Here is an easy strategy to exit a conversation, along with sample phrases that will make exiting a conversation no longer a challenge.

Try using the following three simple steps for exiting a conversation.

Step 1: Say something **positive** about the person or the conversation. For example:

It was really nice talking to you about....   I'd love to continue this conversation....

Try adding some of your own expressions:

_____

_____

Step 2: Indicate **what you need to do** or **where you need to go**. For example:

If you will excuse me, I need to...   I've got to get to a seminar by 2:00 p.m.
I am heading to a class right now,...   I have a class at 1:00 p.m., so please excuse me for rushing.
I have to get to a meeting by 3:00 p.m., but....
Forgive me for being in a rush, but I am really late for an appointment.
Some colleagues are expecting me, so I can't talk right now....

Try adding some of your own expressions:

_____

_____

Step 3: Add one final **positive** comment and leave. For example:

It's really nice to see you again.   We should meet for lunch soon.
We should get together soon.   Let's stay in touch/I will be in touch.
We should get together to chat more about....

Try adding some of your own expressions:

_____

_____

(Note 5)

(E) Making Appointments, Seeking Advice, and Expressing Gratitude   Here are a few
expressions that you might find useful for making appointments, seeking advice, and expressing gratitude.

To make an appointment:

I am calling to make an appointment with you to discuss my research project. I will need about 30 minutes of your time to go through the questions that I have. (Note: It's important to indicate a reasonable amount of meeting time you'll need so that the other person can gauge the amount of detail that he/she needs to provide you in order to adequately address all your questions.)
I know that you have a busy schedule this month. Would you be able to find 20 minutes to see me? I'd like to discuss my upcoming job interview with you.
When might be a convenient day/time for you to see me?
When would you be available to talk to me about...?   Would 1:00 p.m. work for you?

Try adding some of your own expressions:

To request advice:

I would like to seek your guidance on....
Would you advise me how I should go about...?
I have.... Is there anything else that I should do? (It's important to show that you have done your homework and have taken the initiative to be a problem solver.)
What else do you think would help in this situation?
Could you give me some pointers on...?
What recommendations/advice would you give to someone who...?
I am having some trouble interpreting..., and I thought that I would share some of the preliminary findings and my thoughts with you to see if I am on the right track.
I understand that you are the expert in this area/in the area of X. I was hoping that you might explain/help me to understand....

Try adding some of your own expressions:

To express gratitude:

Thank you very much for your advice/suggestions
I am very grateful for your advice.
I (greatly) appreciate your guidance.
I very much/really/greatly appreciate the time that you have taken to....
As always, I appreciate your expert comments and advice.
Thank you for taking the time to read my paper and for your valuable/insightful feedback.
Thanks so much for your helpful advice about....
Thank you once again for taking the time to speak/meet with me the other day.

Try adding some of your own expressions:

2.4 Application Activities

Here are four activities to immediately apply what you have learned in this unit and to monitor your own success along the way.

Activity 1: *Telephoning and meeting with a supervisor*

Part 1: Telephone role-playing

Instructions: Work in pairs and self-select what role to play in the following scenario. Apply the strategies and mechanics introduced in this unit to create and role-play a telephone conversation. When you are ready to carry out the task, sit back-to-back in order to simulate the absence of paralinguistic cues in most telephone conversations. If time permits, switch places so that each person has a chance to play both roles.

Scenario: You call the office of your advisor, Dr. Jones, to make an appointment. Dr. Jones isn't in his office, and you decide to leave a message for him. You call again that same afternoon and are able to speak to Dr. Jones. You ask for an appointment to talk about your research project. Discuss a time when you can meet, and then conclude the conversation.

Worksheet

Greetings + Introduction (Who):

→ Time (When):

→ Purpose (Why):

→ Request (What):

→ Leave your name and/or number (How):

Notes:

_____

_____

_____

(Note. 6)

Part 2: Meeting time

Instructions: If you are playing the role of student, prepare three questions to ask your supervisor. If you are playing the role of adviser, you might like to refer to Section 6.3 (A) *Holding office hours* in your preparation.

Face each other and apply the mechanics introduced in this unit to role-play a meeting that involves seeking and offering advice. Conclude with the student expressing thanks to the supervisor.

Notes:

_____

_____

_____

Activity 2: *Mini-experiment*(For self-study or a take-home task)

When I have asked how much time each day students spend speaking in English with people who are native or fluent speakers of English over my years of teaching, the average is no longer than 20 minutes! Imagine that you can spend no longer than 20 minutes a day working on your doctoral degree or on any subject or skill that you feel passionately about mastering. How long would it take to achieve some success?

Set a mini-goal of striking up one conversation every day for a week with at least three people whom you know or don't know, using the expressions and strategies that you have learned in this unit. This will enhance your comfort level and also promote your fluency and automaticity in engaging in interpersonal communication in academic settings. Don't feel discouraged if you happen to meet someone who doesn't seem to be interested in carrying on a conversation for whatever reason. Don't take it personally. Use the exit lines and simply move on and keep practicing.

Try jotting down some of your thoughts and experiences from this experiment for personal reflection. If you are carrying out this activity as an outside-of-class task, be prepared to share your experience with your class in the following session.

Activity 3: *Conversational ball*(For classroom instruction)

Instructions: Use a ball that is easy to catch and throw for this activity. Divide the class into groups of five. Assign one student to be an observer for each group. (You can also have students volunteer to play the role of observer.) In a circle of no more than five students, one student will ask a question, and then toss the ball to another student who would like to respond to the question. After responding, the student will do the same: ask another question before tossing the ball. Carry on the activity for five minutes to allow the observer to observe the patterns of interactions. If time permits, students in each group will then take turns playing the role of observer.

This activity provides participants an opportunity not only to put what they have learned into practice, but also to learn to monitor others' and one's own communicative interactions. At the end of each round, the observer will briefly report back to the class his/her observations about the group's verbal and nonverbal patterns of interaction, including the use of silence and personal distance. Some other questions that one might ask include: Is there a balanced interaction among the members of a group? Is there a tendency for someone to drop or hog the ball that does not facilitate conversational exchanges?

Observer's notes:

Activity 4: *Let's mingle!*(For classroom instruction)

This is a great activity that simulates situations that graduate students often encounter in departmental gatherings or at conferences and that provides the perfect scenario for learners to practice entering, maintaining, and exiting a conversation.

Prepare a service bell for this activity. This activity has two objectives for the students involved: (a) Using the conversation strategies and phrases in this unit; and (b) making sure that they have a chance to speak to everyone in the class.

Instructions: Ask participants to circulate around the room as they make use of the strategies and phrases in the entering and maintaining a conversation section in this unit. At the sound of the service bell, participants must use the exiting strategies and move on to speak to a new interlocutor. Sound the bell a few times and remind participants to meet with and speak to people whom they haven't yet encountered.

Personal reflection:

- Have you made use of the conversation strategies and phrases introduced in this unit? ☐

- Did you manage to speak to everyone in the class? ☐

- What's one thing that you will try in a similar communication situation?

2.5 Strategies for Success

A. Leaving a phone message: A few "do's and don'ts":

Do:

1. If you know that there is a chance that a machine will answer, then (a) decide beforehand whether you will leave a message, and (b) follow the outline and use the language you have learned.

    > **Greetings** + Introduction (Who) → Time (When) → Purpose (Why) → Request (What) → Leave your name and/or number (How) →**Closing**

2. Say important numbers, names, or addresses slowly and clearly. Repeat them so the recipient of the message won't have to replay the message multiple times.

3. Indicate the priority of the message if necessary.

Don't:

1. Go on forever! Instead, follow the outline, and get to the point.

2. Speak too fast. Don't make people guess what you are saying.

3. Reveal a secret or personal information that you don't wish to share with anyone except the intended receiver.

4. Talk to yourself or others right after you finish the message. Sometimes the recording is still in progress.

5. Chew food or stand next to a television or radio with audible or loud volume.

B. A few pointers on making new acquaintances:

1. Introduce yourself appropriately according to the situation. In formal situations, avoid addressing your professors, supervisors, collaborators, or colleagues casually, even if you know them well personally. In informal situations, convey approachability and keep it simple. Responses may also vary according to the situations, for example, "Nice/Pleased/Pleasure to meet you."

2. If a friend comes along and stops to talk, informally introduce him/her to the person you are talking to. It is helpful to provide some information about each of them, so that each will (a) know what your relationship is to the other person (friend, colleague, instructor, etc.) and (b) have some information (e.g., area of expertise) that can be used to begin a conversation.

3. Avoid speaking in a foreign language in the presence of others who do not understand what is being said.

4. Depending on the context, when you first meet someone, it may be inappropriate to talk about certain things, such as salary, age, religion, political views, illness, the value of someone's belongings, and so on. The discussion in Section 2.2, Facing the Challenges, explains in more detail what sorts of topics should be avoided with new acquaintances.

C. Strategies for maintaining conversations:

Here are simple strategies for keeping the conversational ball rolling as you become familiar with the various commonly used expressions to enter and maintain a conversation and as you develop spontaneity in your follow-up lines in response to the conversation at hand.

1. **Start a new round.** Running out of things to say about the topic at hand? Introduce a new topic (e.g., family, friends, or any of the topics listed in the previous section) through opening lines such as: "What do you think about...?" "Did you hear about...?" "Did I tell you about...?" "Oh, I wanted to ask you about...."

2. **Expand.** Try lengthening the conversation by expanding on the topic. For example, add a few different comments regarding what was just talked about (e.g., by adding facts or information, examples, or your personal experiences and opinions). Many students find that the easiest approach is to relate the conversation to their personal experiences. For example: "What you are saying reminds me of my own experience with...." Linking the conversation to your personal knowledge and experience will help you be more confident, especially in the initial stage of becoming comfortable in sharing thoughts with others and being part of the conversation.

3. **Revisit.** Revisit the information that came up earlier during the conversation but was not elaborated. You will need to exercise active listening skills (see Section 2.5 D, *Practicing active listening skills*) during a conversation so that you know what informational bits you can toss back into the conversation with expressions such as: "You mentioned earlier that you.... Could you tell me more about that?"

4. **Ask, ask, ask!** Questions are used to carry on a conversation. A simple question can keep the conversational ball rolling and can also indicate your interest in continuing it. Being comfortable asking questions can help you establish and maintain relationships in social interactions. Ask open-ended questions (with what, how, why, for example) that usually require your interlocutor to provide more than a simple "yes" or "no" response.

D. Practicing active listening skills:

The importance of practicing active listening skills was noted as a key strategy for maintaining a conversation. Here are six ways to practice active listening skills.

1. **Smile** and maintain good **eye contact** with the person who is talking. (Learn that there are cultural differences in maintaining eye contact. Be aware of how you maintain eye contact with others, and observe how others maintain eye contact with you during a conversation.)

2. **Focus on the speaker.** Don't spend time thinking about what and how you are going to respond to the person. Focusing too much on what you are going to say may hinder your comprehension of the message that the speaker is trying to convey or of the information bits that you can use to maintain the conversation.

3. **Ask questions** or **paraphrase** what you have heard. Active listening includes indicating to your interlocutor that you understood his/her message or feelings. Use response phrases such as the following when you paraphrase or ask questions about what you have just heard: "That sounds (e.g., challenging, [really] interesting, exciting)...." "What happened?" "I see/know what you mean about...." "Let me see if I understood everything. You are saying that...." "Could you provide an example of what you mean by that?" It's important to restate specifics that clarify what others are trying to say to you, to check your understanding of their message, and to let them know that you really heard them. For example: "So you expected X, but you got Y instead, and you are disappointed."

4. **Make listening sounds** (e.g., *uh-huh, mm-hmm, yes, I see, oh really,* etc.). Providing listening sounds or vocal cues is important during interpersonal communication whether in person or over the telephone. These vocal cues, formally called "back-channelling," are ways of indicating to a speaker that you are following and understanding what he/she is saying. They are also used to signal to a speaker that you do not wish to talk even though the speaker may be displaying verbal or nonverbal cues for yielding a turn. (Note: Managing turn-taking conversation will be covered in Unit 4.)

5. **Jot things down.** This is especially applicable when you are meeting with your course instructors or supervisors. Don't keep your head in a notebook; instead, jot down quick notes. This not only indicates to your interlocutor that what he/she is saying is important, but will also help jog your memory about any important information in a conversation.

6. Don't be afraid to ask the person to **repeat** something or to **slow down**. Countless times students have shared stories about their reluctance to ask for repetition because they feel embarrassed about not being able to immediately comprehend what they have heard or think that it would be disrespectful to ask the speaker to repeat the information. As a result, they may have nodded their heads and walked away worrying that they might have missed crucial information that they were supposed to deal with after the conversation. This is not a rare occurrence. Become familiar with various ways to ask for clarification. (Refer to Section 3.3 for more examples.)

UNIT 3

PARTICIPATING IN SMALL GROUP SETTINGS I

3.1 Unit Introduction

Units 3 and 4 center on participation in small group settings, with Unit 3 focusing on building mechanics and strategic competence involved in asking questions and Unit 4 dealing with expressing opinions and managing turns involved in participating in seminars and meetings.

At the graduate level, the importance of participating in small group settings needs no further emphasis. Academic conversation among people who share a common interest helps broaden, strengthen, and deepen their understanding. Not only is one's participation often evaluated as part of a course grade, but one's ability to contribute to the dialogue also will be noted in settings where participation is not being formally evaluated. For example, the quality of your participation in group settings may influence the references that your professors will later write for you in support of your job applications. In addition, the skill you demonstrate at engaging others provides a glimpse into how you deal with others in a group setting. This skill is important because collaborative work in courses and research is on the increase; your professional relationship and ongoing discussions outside the classroom with your fellow classmates, potential collaborators, and future colleagues are also fostered.

The skills involved in participating in small group settings involve a complex set of habits and attitudes that might be deeply ingrained, and, as such, it's important to explore various hidden assumptions related to group participation. This exploration is followed by the coverage of mechanics and strategies pertaining to asking various types of questions. Next are two classroom-tested application activities that promote the development of one's ability to pose questions, and this unit then concludes with some suggestions of strategies for success, including self-introduction to a group, and tips on asking questions and participating effectively in small group settings.

3.2 Facing Challenges and Exploring Hidden Assumptions

Diagnostic questions: Explore these questions on your own if you use this book for self-study. In a classroom, share your thoughts about these questions with a speaking partner and be prepared to share your discussion with the class.

1. If you are using this book in an academic conversation course, you probably have been asked to introduce yourself to your group. If not, you probably have had opportunities to introduce yourself at one of your courses or seminars. How did you do? Did you face any challenges? What challenges did you encounter that other members of your group also faced? If you haven't yet had an opportunity to introduce yourself in a group situation, what sorts of challenges would you anticipate having?

(Note 1)

2. Do you think questioning is important in academic discussions? Why or why not?

3. What do you consider the primary purpose(s) of asking questions? What is your perception of a "good" question? Together, identify some phrases that are used in English to pose various types or levels of questions.

4. From your experience, what types of questions have you noticed in group/seminar discussions? What type(s) have you found to be the most common?

5. What are some of your thoughts arising from your observations of how native speakers of English pose questions as compared with non-native speakers?

6. What are some dimensions of cultural differences that might influence or obstruct how participants with different cultural backgrounds pose questions in small group settings?

(Note 2)

7. How do you feel about your ability to pose questions in academic discussions? What is/are one (or some) of the most challenging aspects of asking questions? Together, brainstorm some strategies that will help you overcome such challenges.

Challenges:

Strategies:

3.3 Mastering the Mechanics of Language

Units 3 and 4 are about participating in group settings, and the language focus here first deals with mastering different types of questions, such as ways of asking for repetition, clarification, and elaboration. This kind of language can be considered as serving functional purposes. Familiarization with the following expressions will free up the thinking time that is needed to generate and formulate the content-based questions as the discussion unfolds moment by moment

Here are some commonly used phrases and expressions that serve various purposes:

(A) Asking for repetition

Some commonly used expressions for requests to someone to repeat are presented here. A simple request for repetition can serve multiple purposes. For example: You might not be 100% sure that you have heard an important point correctly; repetition provides an opportunity to check your understanding. The request might serve as a compensation strategy that buys you some time to think about or formulate your response to the statement just made.

Sorry?/ Pardon me?/ Excuse me?

Would you mind saying/repeating that again?

I'm sorry. I didn't understand what you said about....

Sorry, I didn't (quite) catch what you said.

Sorry, I didn't hear you..../I didn't follow what you said about....

I am having some trouble understanding you. You were saying....

Excuse me, would you mind speaking a little more slowly, please?

I'm sorry. Could you repeat what you said about...?

I'm sorry. Could you repeat the last point you made again?

Try adding some of your own expressions:

(B) Seeking clarification or elaboration

Your participation in small group settings might at some point involve asking someone to explain a point further because there is something that you do not understand.

You mentioned (earlier) that.... Do you mean...?

What did you mean when you said...?

I didn't quite get what you meant by "...."

Could you please be more specific about...?

Could you elaborate on the point you made about...?

Could you explain your second point in more detail...?

You might have already said this, but I wasn't sure what you meant when you said....

I'm not sure what you mean. Do you mean...?

Could you explain what you mean by...?

Sorry, but I'm not (quite) clear on the point you made about....

Could you expand a little bit on what you said about...?

Could you provide an example of...?

Try adding some of your own expressions:

(C) Paraphrasing ideas to confirm understanding

To paraphrase is to say an idea in a different way by, for example, changing key words (e.g., using different word forms, synonyms, and antonyms) and changing the sentence structure (e.g., using active instead of passive sentences). Paraphrasing the point that you wish to address before you advance your own argument ensures that your argument is made based on an accurate understanding and interpretation of what was said. It also shows that you are exercising active listening, as covered in the previous unit.

So what you are saying is that [*paraphrase* the idea].

Please correct me if I have misinterpreted your point. Are you saying that [*paraphrase* the idea]?

So, you mean that [*paraphrase* the idea].

Based on my understanding of the points that you just made, am I correct in assuming that...?

Let me just make sure -- your point is that [*paraphrase* the idea].

If I have understood you correctly, your point is that [*paraphrase* the idea].

The way I understand it, you are saying that [*paraphrase* the idea]. Is that correct?

Try adding some of your own expressions:

(D) Clarifying your comment by putting it in other words

There are times when you can detect that your listeners seem puzzled or lost when they are listening to you. Assume responsibility for your communication, and see that moment as an opportunity for you to clarify your point by expressing it in a different way. The interlocutors' lack of understanding often may not be related to your pronunciation, grammar, or word choice, but to the lack of contextual cues or additional information that help your listeners understand your intended point.

.... I mean....   .... Let me put it another way....
.... To put it another way....   .... In other words, ...
.... What I'm trying to say is....   .... My point is that....
.... The point I'm trying to make is.... .... The point I'm trying to make is....

That's not really what I was asking. My question is about [*paraphrase* the question].

Perhaps I didn't make my question clear. What I asked was[*paraphrase* the question].

I understand your point, but I think you've answered a slightly different question. What I would like to know is [*paraphrase* the question].

Try adding some of your own expressions:

3.4 Application Activities

Activity 1: *Summarizing and sharing opinions*(For classroom instruction)

This activity is designed to promote learners' ability to summarize information, share their summaries verbally, paraphrase summaries they have heard, and elicit and express opinions in a small group setting.

Step 1: Summarizing
Read an assigned article and underline five sentences that you think are the most important. Then try combining them into two to three sentences. In your own words, summarize the article. (This exercise is also suitable for self-study.)

Step 2: Sharing
In pairs, take turns presenting a very brief summary of the article that each person has chosen. The other person will paraphrase on the basis of the summary given by the other student.

Step 3: Sharing opinions
Use the expressions learned in this unit to (a) check everyone's understandings of one another's summaries if they are different, (b) practice eliciting opinions about the main issues of the article, and (c) discuss the issues.

Activity 2: *Questions, questions, and more questions*(For classroom instruction)

The following article titled "Practicing speaking for academic purposes using Aristotle's *Topics*" was published in *Communication Teacher*. The first part of the article provides background material to help instructors introduce the use of Aristotle's *topics* as a speaking strategy that will enable learners to develop academic speaking skills applicable to individual presentations, seminars, and group discussions. This is followed by a detailed description of the activity that puts the strategy into action.

Practicing Speaking for Academic Purposes Using Aristotle's *Topics*

Objective: To expand advanced second language learners' speaking repertoires and promote communicative competence

Course: Advanced Speaking for Academic Purposes

In my years of teaching Advanced English for Academic Purposes across disciplines at the postsecondary and graduate levels, I have found that many advanced second language learners have difficulty speaking in academic settings and express a strong desire to be part of the dialogue. This observation has been supported by several studies, which have shown that participating in seminars and expressing themselves in speech are among the top challenges that second language graduate and undergraduate student learners face in academic settings (see Jordan, 1997). Faculty members also have noted that second language learners need to improve their oral communication skills in class discussions and presentations (e.g., Zhu & Flaitz, 2005). For advanced, international graduate students, linguistic and paralinguistic issues and discipline-specific, discourse-level conventions certainly come into play, but many such learners still lack the necessary experience or confidence to speak in various academic settings and find it difficult to cope with the pressing need to formulate a contribution quickly (e.g., "I can't think what to say") and feel uncertain about their contributions' value (e.g., "I might say something that sounds unintelligent"). These challenges present a major stumbling block to their taking part in discourse communities. The teaching activity presented here introduces the use of Aristotle's *topics* as a speaking strategy that can help advanced second language learners develop confidence in their abilities to make individual presentations and/or to make dialogical contributions to group discussions, seminars, or academic debates.

A Brief Note on Aristotle's *Topics*
During the fourth century B.C., Aristotle developed the *topics* to help his students discover what could be used to develop a subject. Since then, Aristotle's *topics* been borrowed and put to great use in various disciplines and in the teaching of academic writing. The *topics*, in Greek "topoi" or in Latin "loci" (words that mean "places"), are conceived as places where ideas can be assigned within categories or classifications, or under headings. This process can help speakers

and writers invent ideas and group relevant material to develop a subject. Aristotle distinguished between *common topics*, which are general and can be used for any science, and *special topics*, which can be applied to either a particular science or a particular type of oratory. Table 1 lists five *common topics* (definition, comparison, relationship, circumstance, testimony) and two *special topics* (judicial and deliberative); these are accompanied by some questions to help students create situational examples that might enhance their thinking/research. For the original discussion on the *topics*, refer to Aristotle's *Rhetoric* (1954), and for a detailed description and discussion of each *topic*, see Corbett and Connors (1999).

Table 1 Handout: Aristotle's *Topics*[1]

Issue:

Common/Special *Topics*	Questions (Examples)
Definition ▪ Genus ▪ Division	▪ How does the dictionary define X (e.g., the topic)? ▪ What do I mean by X? ▪ To what group of things does X belong? ▪ Into what parts can X be divided? ▪ What other words mean the same as X? ▪ When is the meaning of X misunderstood?
Comparison ▪ Similarity ▪ Difference ▪ Degree	▪ What characteristics does X share with others? In what ways? ▪ From what is X different? In what ways? ▪ How significant are those similarities and/or differences?
Relationship ▪ Cause and effect ▪ Antecedent and consequence ▪ Contraries ▪ Contradictions	▪ What causes X? What makes X happen? ▪ What are the effects of X? ▪ What is/are the consequence(s) of X? ▪ What comes before/after X? ▪ What is the opposite of X? ▪ What other interpretations could there be of X?
Circumstance ▪ Possible or impossible ▪ Past fact and future fact	▪ How feasible/possible is X? What can or cannot happen? ▪ What factors make X either possible or impossible? ▪ What precedents are there for X? ▪ Has X happened before? ▪ Based on past experience, what can you predict for the future of X, or for the future of something else if X happens? What will or will not happen?
Testimony/Evidence ▪ Authority ▪ Testimonial ▪ Statistics ▪ Maxims/proverbs ▪ Law ▪ Precedents (examples)	▪ What authorities can you cite? ▪ Who has personally experienced X? How might their experience lend to the credibility of your position on X? ▪ What are some documented facts in statistics/research about X? ▪ What commonly accepted sayings are applicable to X? ▪ What established laws or policies govern X? ▪ What previous incidents of X can you cite?

---

1. The last special *topic*, "ceremonial," which includes such discourses as political speeches, graduation speeches, funeral orations, celebratory speeches, and remarks by emcees, is not included here because it is not used often in this teaching/learning context.

Common/Special Topics	Questions (Examples)
Judicial • Justice/injustice	• Is X just or unjust? What is just or unjust about X?
Deliberative • Good or bad • Worthy or unworthy • Advantageous or disadvantageous	• Is X good or bad? • Is X advantageous or disadvantageous? • What advantages or disadvantages might accrue because of X? • To whom is X advantageous or disadvantageous?

The Activity

The average working time for procedural steps one to five (see below) may vary from 90 to 120 minutes, depending on the issue under discussion, the size of the class, how the class is divided into groups, and the allotted time.

1. Allow 20 to 30 minutes to introduce Aristotle's *topics* and their application to learners. Use the handout provided above, and choose an example that would be interesting to the students or ask the class to come up with a suitable, non-field-specific subject. Use a brainstorm method to facilitate learners' thinking and to elicit their responses as the whole class goes through the list of possible questions for each *topic* listed in Table 1. Write down students' contributions in point form on a flip chart, overhead transparency, or the board. The exercise also will illustrate that not all of Aristotle's *topics* suitable for discussing any particular subject/issue.

For example, take the use of the journal impact factor as a measure of journal quality--an issue of great interest to graduate students, particularly those in the hard sciences. An impact factor is a measure that reflects the frequency with which a journal's articles are cited in the scientific literature by calculating the total number of citations a journal's papers receive, and dividing it by the number of papers the journal publishes. Some perceive the impact factor as an indication of a journal's prestige or quality, while others have proposed different methods to quantify the cumulative impact and relevance of one's research output. These include, for example, the *PageRank*, which assigns importance ranks to nodes in a linked database of documents containing citations, and the *h-index*, which is used to quantify researchers' productivity based on their publication records by calculating the number of times a researcher's publications are cited in other papers. The class can explore the differences among these measures, what brings about the use of an impact factor, the consequences of using it, its validity, who has personally experienced its use in their publication or job search endeavours, the pros and cons of using such a measure in evaluating scientific journals, hiring, promotions, and grants, for whom the use of such measure is advantageous or disadvantageous, and so on.

2. Distribute several flashcards prepared in advance, with each listing a debatable issue (e.g., genetically modified foods, stem cell research, the two-tier health care system, euthanasia, organ sales, same-sex marriage, the impact factor in scientific publications) and a suitable *topic* (e.g., circumstance, comparison, testimony/evidence). For an extensive list of debatable issues, refer to Sather (1999).

3. Ask learners to work in small groups. One person draws a card out of a hat for the group, and each group has 5 to 10 minutes to generate thoughts and respond to the prompt.

4. Reconvene the class for a two- to three-minute presentation of each group's points. The presentation length and format (e.g., individual or group) can vary, depending on the *topic*, the allocated time, and the class size. After each group's presentation, allow some time for learners to raise any questions and for a whole class discussion.

5. To wrap up, the instructor might summarize the key points generated by using appropriate *topics* to talk about the different issues. The instructor also could assign two students at the beginning of the activity to play the role of summarizers, who would be responsible for providing the key points generated from all groups.

Debriefing

After the whole class discussion or the individual presentations, the students should discuss the process, as well as the product of using Aristotle's *topics* to develop and deliver their talks. Some questions the instructor might want to ask include the following:

1. What did you learn from the process of preparing for your talk?
2. What challenges did you encounter when you were completing the activity?
3. What did you learn about the *topics* or issue from the discussions/presentations?
4. How did completing this activity differ from how you usually prepare for class discussions or brief talks?
5. What speaking strategies did you employ to help you deliver your ideas? Which strategies were useful for you and which were not?
6. What worked and what did not work in terms of using the *topics* to develop your talk?

Variations:

1. Instead of preparing debatable topics, instructors might ask students to prepare for the class by selecting a major newspaper and identifying current issues about which people have different opinions. Spend 10 to 15 minutes together in the previous class generating a list of possible issues that would be suitable[2] for debate/discussion, based on the issues identified. I also regularly gather articles from journals and newspapers about topics that I consider suitable for various speaking tasks (e.g., discussions, debates, presentations). Give learners two articles that display opposing views on the same issue and assign them as required readings for the upcoming session.

2. As a follow-up/reinforcement activity for the next class, distribute a handout of the table, but with a blank right column where learners can fill in their thoughts and/or the information gathered. Assign students an issue about which they will gather thoughts and/or information. Then use the pyramid approach. That is: (a) allow 10 minutes for learners to work first **individually** by going through the *topics* to produce a list of tentative ideas; (b) request that learners work in **small groups** for 15 to 20 minutes, as they share and help each other discover the meanings that others are trying to express, and also to use others' diverse insights and perspectives to advance their own understanding of the issue; and (c) proceed with a 20- to 30-minute **whole class** discussion or informal debate.

3. An alternative follow-up activity is to have students prepare a three-minute persuasive talk for the next class. Encourage learners to self-select an issue and utilize the handout of Aristotle's *topics* to help them uncover, discover, and organize their thoughts, ideas, and information. The instructor also could generate a list of current debatable or controversial issue from which the learners can select. The three-minute time limit and the self-selection of an issue make the speaking task more manageable for students. In addition, the task compels learners to practice being concise. This alternative activity provides everyone with an opportunity to practice; it leaves no one out because of individual differences.

Appraisal

This activity can be used as a confidence-building, non-graded activity during the early stage of an oral communication or oral presentation course or as a graded activity where both process (i.e., group/whole class participation) and product (e.g., individual talks or group presentations) are assessed. The grading criteria for this activity will vary, depending on the teaching and learning objective(s) and the criteria that course instructors develop.

Having been adapted by instructors in various disciplines over many years, Aristotle's *topics* have retained their original, heuristic value, inviting students to more deeply consider issues using a communicative pedagogy. In my teaching of Advanced Speaking for Academic Purposes, Aristotle's *topics* been a useful mediating tool that helps learners tap into their existing knowledge and identify what can be said or what kinds of information can be used to talk about or discuss a subject. The various *topics* serve as prompts for helping learners discover *how much they already know* about a given issue based on their experience, education, reading, and reflection. Furthermore, when learners have just a few bits and pieces of scrambled ideas, or when more thorough research of an issue is required for a longer presentation, the *topics* provide structures for exploring, generating, and recreating new ideas and thoughts. With practice, learners will be able to

---

2. The criteria I use to determine issue suitability include current relevance (i.e., an issue that is of current interest to the academic community or the general public), level (i.e., an issue that students from various disciplines can understand and discuss), value (i.e., an issue that will be of value to participants because it provides opportunities to learn divergent viewpoints and to demonstrate analytical and problem-solving skills), range (i.e., an issue that can generate a wealth of responses using the *topics*), interest (i.e., an issue that participants would find interesting to discuss), balance (i.e., an issue that includes plenty of arguments supporting various sides), and resolution (i.e., an issue that should generate numerous potential solutions that could be debated).

run quickly through the *topics* mentally to identify points that could be made about the subject or issue at hand. They also can use them to explore, broaden, and challenge their original thinking and enhance their ability and confidence to present shorter comments or longer presentations on any subject. Practicing various speaking activities utilizing the *topics* further promotes language learning and development.

Activity 3: *Panel discussion* (For classroom instruction)

Instructions: Assign an article that has current relevance to the academic community or a research article that students from various disciplines can understand and discuss. Divide the class into three groups. One group will represent the experts; one will be the questioners; and the third will be the observers.

Preparation Period (20 minutes):

Expert Group: Read the article and anticipate questions that the Questioner Group might raise. Group members might consider designating different members to be responsible for responding to certain aspects of the article (e.g., the methodology, findings, interpretation, recommendations, and so on) so that the group can ensure that there is a balance in participation and contributions among members.

Questioner Group: The first step is for individuals to generate a few questions about the article. Then gather as a group to select a list of questions to pose to the Expert Group. Include some questions that challenge the Expert Group's position, if such questions are appropriate to the situation. Make sure that there are questions from different levels and various foci, and revise them to enhance the clarity and focus, if necessary.

Observer Group: Divide the group into two subgroups. One will observe the Expert Group members' interactions during the group activity, and the other will observe the Questioner Group members' interactions. Group members will take notes about what they have observed. (Be observant of the nature of your group's contributions by reflecting on such questions as: Was there a balanced interaction among the participants? What sorts of questions were posed? What type(s) of questions were the most common? Did certain types of comments often get made? Were participants' comments challenging each other in a constructive way?)

Question Period (30 minutes):

Start the question period much like a press conference that you would see on television. The Observer Group will continue to observe participants' verbal and nonverbal language, and to make notes of the exchanges and interactions in the session as a whole. Once the question period is complete, the Expert and Questioner Groups will reflect on their performance by using the appropriate checklists for reflection provided in the following section (Section 3.5 B and C). The two observer subgroups will come together to share their observations and notes, and be prepared to report their findings back to the class. Members of the Expert and Questioner Groups are also invited to respond or share their thoughts and personal reflections.

(Note 3)

3.5 Strategies for Success

A. Introducing oneself to a group:

When it comes to academic conversation in small group settings, the first potential challenge that many students face is self-introduction in a group situation. As the instructor goes around the room or while you are waiting for your turn, your heart may start pounding, your palms may get sweaty, your tongue may get dry, and your breath may become shallow. This seemingly easy situation actually has all the ingredients that increase apprehension for most people: the formality of the situation, the anticipation of your turn coming up, the feeling of wanting to escape from the situation, the time pressure that you might be under, and becoming the centre of the attention among an unfamiliar group of people and in unfamiliar surroundings. Here is an easy-to-follow plan for you to get ready to put your best foot forward in creating the right impression when you introduce yourself to a group.

1. Recognize that it is **normal** to feel nervous. You are not alone.

2. **Plan a simple sequence** for introducing yourself. Here are two sample sequences:

    a. Say your name slowly. Note that you are familiar with your name, but others may not be: I'm…. My name is ….
        Next, say the main thing you want others to know: e.g., I'm here to….
        Conclude: e.g., I'm looking forward to....

    b. State your name, position, and affiliation.
        Say where you are from and how long you have been in the country.
        State the main thing you would like others to know.
        Share any other relevant piece of information about yourself.
        Conclude.

3. Take a few **deep breaths** while waiting to speak.

4. **Start speaking after you inhale** and not after you exhale. Starting to speak after you exhale creates a shortness of breath that can exacerbate the nervousness or anxiety associated with speaking.

5. **Smile** and use **a relaxed posture** to convey approachability.

6. Try making **eye contact** with people in all corners of the room throughout your introduction.

7. **End confidently**. Avoid the temptation to end your introduction as soon as you can or to use weak exits such as: "Well, I guess that's it." or "Um, that's all…."

B. Tips on asking questions:

☐ **Be the first to ask a question**. Many students share the sentiments of fear and anxiety about asking a question that may sound "stupid" to others. Be the first to raise a question because, as the discussion progresses, participation often becomes increasingly complex and difficult if you are new to this academic practice. After you have asked a question, you will often feel more at ease and involved, and, gradually, your confidence about raising questions will be enhanced through the successful small steps that you have made.

☐ You need to **exercise effective listening skills** (review Unit 2, Section 2.5 D) so that you can ask questions that are related to the comments being made or to the subject being discussed, i.e., questions that are important to developing the discussion.

☐ **Prepare questions in advance**. Being able to pose questions that facilitate the flow of discussion by exercising effective listening skills and to sharply question assigned materials in seminar discussions contribute to group members' learning. To that end, commit to preparing some good questions. (Consider different types of questioning, and ask questions that reflect reason, focus, and clarity.) The key to effective discussion is preparation. The more prepared you are, the less apprehensive you will feel about participating. You will also get more out of the discussion.

☐ **Be precise** (i.e., to the point) and **concise** (i.e., brief) in your questions. Avoid rambling on and on or taking too long to get to the point if that tends to be your conversational style.

☐ Use **words that come naturally** to you. When you participate in academic discussion in your department, focus your attention on getting your message and idea across. Focus on speaking to express rather than impress.

☐ You need to use **appropriate intonation**. If you are asking someone a question that challenges the person's comments, make sure that you don't elevate your voice or sound like you are attacking the person.

(Note 4)

C. More tips on participating in small group settings:

When you are trying to persuade your audience in a discussion, it is important that you try not to be combative. Try to understand other points of view and keep in mind the following points:

☐ Establish credibility or believability with the audience. You are considered reliable if you are knowledgeable on all sides of the issue. One of the ways to become knowledgeable is **to be prepared**. Do all the readings and, whenever possible, go beyond the readings on the topic.

☐ **Never confuse fact with opinion!** Understand the underlying complexity of issues, and do not simply take things for granted because *"that's just the way it is."*

☐ Provide **well-established evidence** that relates to the issue under discussion. Make sure that the evidence you present is well supported in the literature and that your conclusions are based on the facts you provide. Studies have shown that others are much more likely to be influenced by a statement of facts that explains *"This is why I came to the conclusion I reached."*

☐ Provide answers and present your arguments in **a logical sequence**. Many students have found that jotting down key words for each point and numbering them help accomplish that goal.

☐ **Show enthusiasm.** Your audience/listeners will be more interested if they see your enthusiasm.

☐ Defend your position when justified, but **don't get defensive**.

☐ Let the other person state his/her case and listen to his/her point of view. In expressing disagreement, **avoid interrupting** someone before he/she is finished.

☐ **Be willing to make changes in your point of view** based on new information.

(Note 5)

UNIT 4

PARTICIPATING IN SMALL GROUP SETTINGS II

4.1 Unit Introduction

This unit builds on the content covered in previous units and continues to develop the more advanced communication skills that involve expressing opinions and managing turn-taking. Group discussions provide opportunities for us to learn from the insights of others, and we can develop a view that is much wider or deeper than one we arrived at by ourselves. Engaging in seminars productively, however, involves skills beyond fluency in English. Productive engagement requires one to, for example, listen attentively, to build on previous comments made by others, to help discover the meaning that others may be struggling to articulate, to substantiate claims with reasons or evidence, to use others' perspectives and insights to advance one's own understanding of the issue under discussion, to be open to diverse viewpoints, and to address others and their arguments respectfully.

With these goals in mind, we next explore communication challenges and the operation of hidden assumptions in expressing opinions and managing turn-taking. This exploration is followed by coverage of both verbal and nonverbal mechanics in those aspects of communication, which you can apply immediately to get started on expanding your linguistic and strategic repertoires, stretching your comfort zones, and building your confidence in becoming involved in an academic community. The inclusion of classroom-tested pedagogical activities aims to help you apply the mechanics you've learned. Finally, the Strategies for Success section provides suggestions about how to take control of your talk in turn-taking situations and how to engage in seminars or discussions productively.

4.2 Facing Challenges and Exploring Hidden Assumptions

Diagnostic questions: Explore these questions on your own if you use this book for self-study. In a classroom, share your thoughts about these questions with a speaking partner and be prepared to share your discussion with the class.

1. How do you distinguish among fact, opinion, belief, prejudice, and stereotype? Together, come up with a statement about each of them. Why is understanding these terms important in the context of academic dialogues or discussions?

    Fact:

    Opinion:

    Belief:

    Prejudice:

    Stereotype:

2. (a) What does academic freedom mean to you? (b) Do you give your own opinions in classroom discussions? If not, why not? (c) How do you feel about your ability to express agreement and disagreement in academic discussions versus in interpersonal communications? (d) What are some personal difficulties that you face in offering your agreement/disagreement when you participate in seminar discussions?

    (a)

    (b)

    (c)

    (d)

    (Note 1)

3. What are some dimensions of cultural differences that may influence or create an obstacle in how, for example, professor/student and student/student with different cultural backgrounds interact and communicate in expressing opinions?

4. Share with your speaking partner(s) how you express agreement, disagreement, and partial agreement. Together, write down as many ways as you can remember of stating your opinion, agreement, disagreement, and partial agreement about an issue for discussion.

    Agreement:

    Disagreement:

    Partial Agreement:

5. What is turn-taking and why does it matter?

6. Share with your group member(s) your personal/cultural perception/interpretation of interruption in interpersonal conversation/academic discussions. Consider cross-cultural differences. What factors may come into play in turn-taking?

(Note 2)

7. How do you know when it is your turn to talk in a conversation? What kinds of verbal and nonverbal signals have you noticed being used in turn-taking in academic discussions that seem different from the customs in your country?

    Verbal signals:

    Nonverbal signals:

8. What are the two biggest challenges that you and your group member(s) shared in dealing with taking a turn at speaking in academic discussions/interpersonal communications? Brainstorm some strategies that will help you to overcome them and prepare to share them with the class.

    Challenges:

    Strategies:

4.3 Mastering the Mechanics of Language

(A) Expressing an opinion

There are many occasions when you will want to express your opinion, or when supervisors or colleagues will ask you for it in meetings, seminars, or conversations. Here are some common expressions to get you started on stating your opinion about a subject.

I think that....	I (strongly) believe that....
As I see it....	My opinion about this topic is that....
In my opinion....	From my perspective....
It seems to me that....	In my view....
My point of view is that....	If it is the case that..., then....
It may be/could be argued/maintained that....	It has been argued/said that....

Try adding some of your own expressions:

_____

_____

(B) Agreeing and disagreeing

When you are having a discussion, it is alright to disagree with someone else's ideas/opinions, but it is important to be **tactful** when you are disagreeing. Being tactful means disagreeing with someone else's ideas without offending or insulting that person. Familiarize yourself with the following expressions for stating agreement, disagreement, and partial agreement. These expressions allow you to focus on your reasons, not on the position. Note that sometimes speakers may go directly to the point without explicitly using the expressions that state agreement and disagreement.

To express agreement:

I (totally/completely/quite) agree with you.	That's (exactly) what I think.
That's what I think too.	I think that's a very good point.
My viewpoint is in congruent with yours -- that....	I couldn't agree with you more on....
On the whole, I think your arguments are fair.	That's an excellent point.
[Group] After discussing..., we all agreed that....	

To express disagreement

that, after you state your response, listeners may expect you to provide reasons and evidence to support it. You may choose to respond in ways that range from tactfully indirect to tactfully direct.

I disagree (with you) because....	I'm not sure I agree with this idea/with you on that....
I'm not sure that I entirely agree with you because....	Should we consider the fact that...?
With all due respect, however, I wonder if....	I think your idea is plausible, but I would argue that....
I understand your point, but the evidence suggests that....	A counter-example would be....

Perhaps there is another way of looking at this issue -- for instance....

With all due respect to [e.g., Dr. X and his work], I wish to point out that....

There remains the problem of....

As insightful as the point may be, it does not address the issue at hand.

To express partial agreement, doubt, or reservation:

You can indirectly signal a disagreement or an alternative by acknowledging the value of a particular viewpoint. The use of words such as "may," "seem," or "appear," or adjectives (or adverbs), such as "reasonable," "justifiable," and "plausible," to qualify a statement are common in acknowledgements.

I agree with you to a certain extent, but studies suggest that....

Yes, that may be true/you may be right, but research shows that....

I see what you mean (what you are saying), but the evidence supports the conclusion that....

I understand where you are coming from, but research findings indicate that....

I agree with you that..., but maybe we should look at this issue another way....

I agree with the statement that..., but if we look at the issue from a different angle....

The claims that Brown made may have some merit, but on closer examination....
The evidence presented (might/may/seem to) (suggest/indicate/point to/lead one to think) that....
[Name] has made a plausible case to support..., but one (could/can/might/may) argue that....
What [name] (claims/suggests/asserts) may be (true/a valid point), but ... cannot be overlooked.

Try adding some of your own expressions:

(C) Participating in/leading seminars or meetings

To contribute an additional point:

To bring up another point....

Another interesting point is....

What you have just said reminded me of....

Further to everyone's comments, I'd like to add another point, if I may.

I have one additional thought....

[*Name*]'s comments are very insightful. They led me to....

Following up on [*name*]'s comments....

To emphasize a point:

It seems to me that the real issue is....

As I see it, the most important point/issue is....

In my opinion, the main problem/central issue is....

I think that we cannot overlook the importance of....

To ask others for opinions:

What's your position on....

[Name], I wonder if you'd like to comment on....

[Name], would you like to give us your opinion on/about....

[Name], what's your reaction to....

To wrap up a discussion:

Let me summarize what we have talked about.

We are just about out of time. Let me conclude by saying....

Are there any final thoughts on this issue before we wrap up for the day?

Try adding some of your own expressions:

(D) Taking turns speaking

Non-verbal and vocal mechanics

Turn-yielding cues: Turn-yielding cues are used by speakers to let listener(s) know that they have finished what they want to say. Turn-yielding cues may be transmitted via the following signals, for example: intonation, expressions such as "you know," a drop in pitch/loudness, completion of a grammatical clause, unfilled pauses, the termination of hand gestures, the relaxation of body position, the resumption of a gaze towards the listener, the turning of the head toward the discussion leader, and so on.

Turn-maintaining cues: Turn-maintaining cues, in which speaking-turn requests are suppressed, are used by speakers to keep their speaking turns. Hand gestures may be the most common nonverbal cues used for this purpose. Some vocal cues may be used to accompany hand gestures. Examples of vocal cues may include: changes in volume, increased rate of speech in response to turn-requesting cues from listeners, the use of more filled pauses (e.g., *ah... um...*) that eliminate silent pauses.

Turn-requesting cues: Turn-requesting is more frequently accomplished by simultaneous talking or overlapping talk. This may include short, content-free words or phrases, such as *"but uh...."* This constitutes a clear attempt/request by the listener to talk or to show that he/she wants to talk next. Such words may be uttered by the turn seeker while the speaker is talking or while the speaker is silent, either during a pause or after the speaker has clearly ended his/her utterance.

Nonverbal signals: Be observant of the following examples of nonverbal cues that people use in managing turn-taking. Do people in your culture use similar nonverbal signals when they participate in group settings? It's important to be aware of any cross-cultural differences in habitual visual turn-taking cues that you or others may use.

- ☐ head nodding as a turn-taking signal?
- ☐ blinking eyes as a turn-taking signal?
- ☐ using eyebrow movement to signal turn-taking?
- ☐ using eye contact or gaze for conversation turn management?
- ☐ hand gesticulation?
- ☐ shifting or relaxation of posture or body position?
- ☐ turning of the head toward a speaker?
- ☐ raising hands?
- ☐ using an index finger?
- ☐ standing up?

Verbal mechanics

To interrupt politely and prevent interruptions: To indicate that you want to speak, you can use nonverbal signals such as **leaning forward** or **raising your hand**. You can also gain the attention of the group **during a pause** by using the following phrases:

May (Could) I ask a question?	May (Could) I say something, please?
May (Could) I make a suggestion?	I have a point I'd like to make.
Excuse me for interrupting, but....	Sorry to interrupt, but....
If I could just come in here....	If I could add another point here....
If I may suggest another explanation....	Can I make a quick comment about that?

To keep your turn:

Could you let me finish my thought, please?	I need a little more time to finish up this thought.
Excuse me, I'd like to finish this point.	Wait, I'm just about to finish my point.

(Note: Watch your tone to avoid sounding hostile, especially in a heated discussion.)

To continue after an interruption:

As I was saying....	As I mentioned earlier....
Going back to what I was saying....	Going back to the point that I was making....

[Discussion leading] To manage turn-taking when too many people talk at the same time:

Let's have one person at a time speak, please....   Let's listen to what [name] has to say....
Why don't we let [name] go first? Then, [name] can speak next.... It's your turn, [name].

Try adding some of your own expressions:

_____

_____

_____

4.4 Application Activities

Activity 1: *Pyramid discussions*(For classroom instruction)

A pyramid discussion is a method whereby participants are encouraged to engage in discussion while gradually increasing the group size, starting with working individually, then working in pairs, and then in groups of 3 or 4 before gathering the groups for a whole class discussion. Here is an example of the steps that you may want to take:

Steps:

1. Individually generate choices about the three biggest challenges for non-English-speaking international graduate students studying in a North American academic institution.

    My choices: 1.

    2.

    3.

2. Work in pairs. Share and discuss your personal choices and then decide the top three choices and their ranking.

    Our choices: 1.

    2.

    3.

3. After the pair discussion, form a group of 4 to share your updated top three choices and then together decide on how the choices should be ranked.

    Our group's choices: 1.

    2.

    3.

4. Bring the groups together to elicit each group's top three choices. Each group should take turn calling out the numbers of its choices. Write the top three choices from each group on the board for all to see.

5. In groups of 4 from step 3, prepare arguments to defend your group's choices in order to persuade other groups to make changes in their choices. (Time: 10 minutes)

6. Gather the groups for a whole class discussion. Remind the participants to apply the mechanics and strategies for expressing opinions. (Time: 20 minutes)

(Note 3)

Activity 2: *Informal debate -- Take 1*(For classroom instruction)

In discussions, it's important to be able to express your opinion clearly and, most importantly, to support your argument with reasons, examples, or evidence. The following article titled "Debate as a pathway to academic discussion," which was published in *TESOL Journal*, provides a detailed procedural description of an informal debate activity.

The model outlined here presents one of the speaking activities designed to facilitate learners' development of advanced speaking skills that are needed in academic discussion. This facilitation is accomplished through an informal debating format aimed at familiarizing learners with the language used in expressing opinion and also at fostering learners' critical thinking and speaking. The activity has worked well in the undergraduate ESL and graduate level EAP courses that I am teaching. The average working time may range from 60 to 120 minutes, depending on factors such as the topic, the class size, and the time allocated for whole class discussions. I found that, after a few rounds of guided practice, both the quantity and the quality of learners' verbal output were enhanced. Learners also expressed that they felt more comfortable and confident about participating in the discussions and in ongoing dialogues within the academic community – i.e., in areas where they previously often felt incapable of participating and experienced a great sense of frustration.

Procedure

1. Facilitate a 10 to 15 minute brainstorming session to elicit expressions useful for stating opinions, agreement, disagreement, and partial agreement. You may write down expressions contributed by learners on the board or on an overhead, which later can be used as a reference tool for learners in their application of those expressions.
2. Explain to the learners that this activity will be devoted to a critical discussion of the "pros" and "cons" of a specific current issue. It is important to clarify that the format of this debate does not follow the formal rules of a debate, in which comments are judged and one side is declared the winner against the other. Point out that the purpose of this informal debate is for the learners to practice expressing opinions and engaging in the exchange of ideas. The goal is to develop a broader view through the exploration and consideration of different perspectives on an issue. Instruct the learners to (a) concentrate on reasons and not positions – that is, to explain their own reasons for a position and question the other person in order to discover the reasons behind the differences and address them respectfully; (b) respect others' viewpoints by listening attentively to each point or counter-argument, and by not interrupting the objections or explanations of the other person; (c) use the diverse insights and perspectives of others to advance their own understanding.
3. Show the learners the topic (or it could be a headline of a newspaper or journal article) and spend a few minutes in a warm up discussion, eliciting what they think the issue/debate is. For an extensive list of topics and a brief one to two pages of the arguments for and against each topic/subject, refer to Sather (1999). Here are some topic suggestions that worked well in my graduate level EAP classroom:
   - Non-native international graduate students as teaching assistants (advantages vs. disadvantages)
   - Does the world need genetically modified foods? (risks vs. benefits)
   - Should organ sales be legalized or banned?
4. Ask the learners to work in pairs. Give the learners 10 to 15 minutes to perform a "pros/cons" analysis of the issue by filling in the chart provided. Remind learners the importance of concentrating on reasons and not positions, and of finding out the reasons behind the differences when there is a difference of opinion.

Issue	Pros	Cons
Supporting Points Reasoning/Evidence		

5. Randomly divide the class into two groups: "pros" and "cons," or have a quick poll regarding participants' positions on the chosen issue. If there is a roughly 50-50 split, ask learners to form a team with those who share the same opinion. Then you may assign the "pro" group members to present the pro side or its opposite. Encouraging learners to represent the opposite of their opinion provides opportunities for learners to think critically. It helps to develop their abilities to think outside the box, by considering a different perspective and by examining an issue from both sides.

6. Give the learners 10 minutes to solidify reasons for their position as well as to consider their responses to possible arguments that the opposing side may present. Encourage the learners to jot down key words/points that may help them present their ideas and arguments. You may provide copies of the following sheet to help the learners formulate their talk/response.

Introduction (Main Point)	Body (Supporting Points)		Conclusion (Summarizing Point)
	Reasons/examples	Order to be presented	
	➤	☐	
	➤	☐	
	➤	☐	

7. Begin a 20 to 30 minute debate by asking a willing member of the "pro" side to present one of the arguments. Allow any member of the "con" side to reply. Then let the discussion flow according to the ideas being presented. Allow learners to discuss their ideas freely and exchange their arguments as each point emerges. Expect this informal debate to be lively, and allow both sides to play their roles as advocates or opponents of the particular issue at hand. Make sure that there is a broad and balanced discussion by participants. You may interrupt students who tend to dominate the discussion tactfully by saying something like: *"[Name], you touched on some very important points on this issue, and I know that you have a lot of points to add, but before we hear them, let's get some input from other members. Does someone else want to comment on the issue or on what has been said so far?"* Call on the shyer ones in an encouraging way: *"[Name], I noticed that you wrote down some points earlier. What do you have?"* If you adhere to the principle that everyone must participate through verbal output, you may try a method that I have used that has worked well for increasing student participation. Distribute a simple mini-check list where students must, for example, make two statements, with at least one counter-argument, by the end of the discussion period. Students return their check lists at the end of the class, and this allows me to keep track of learners' participation, and to provide feedback and encouragement. This strategy also has the benefit of limiting those who monopolize and encouraging the quiet ones.
8. Provide learners five minutes to consolidate arguments and prepare brief speeches summarizing their cases. Each side will nominate a person or ask one volunteer to summarize the team's key points of view, following the simple format of Position (one sentence) – Supporting points (select no more than three key supporting points) – Conclusion (one sentence).
9. Wrap up the activity with a request to the learners to self-reflect individually for three to five minutes on their participation by answering and sharing the following questions: (1) What do I like about my participation today? (2) Did I experience any difficulty in expressing myself today? If so, what was it? (3) What is one thing that I can do to help me more successfully convey my thoughts next time?

Alternatives

Variation of Step 1: When learners can't seem to come up with any phrases other than "I think...," "I agree...," and "I disagree...," I have found that it is very productive to distribute a handout such as the one provided here. Introduce some sample expressions and ask the learners to work in small groups to brainstorm and add to the list. Ask each group to share with the class what it has generated. This serves as an opportunity for correction when necessary, for reinforcement through repetition, and for learners to add what further items they have to the list. Wrap up by reminding learners to experiment with expressions during the speaking activity.

Variations of Step 3: (a) Instead of assigning learners a topic, you may prepare a list of topics and allow learners to choose a topic that appeals to them the most. Alternatively, you could spend a few minutes in the previous class on generating together a topic of interest shared by the majority. This suggestion is based on my belief and experience that a productive discussion requires careful planning; at the same time, flexibility and spontaneity can permeate the progression of the discussion in the class. (b) I regularly gather articles from journals and newspapers about topics/subjects that I consider suitable for class debate. Give out to all learners two articles that display opposing views or perspectives on the same issue. If the texts are lengthy, you may give the learners both articles in the previous session and assign them as required readings for the upcoming session. If the texts are relatively short, allow a few minutes reading time in class.

Variations of Step 8: You may establish in advance that, at the end of the discussion, each side will nominate the person who speaks the least to summarize. Positively point out that it is because the person is a great "listener!" This will motivate the quiet ones, who are tentative about their ideas or prefer more thinking time instead of an off-the-cuff response, to (a) participate during the discussion if they do not wish to summarize the case, or (b) be prepared for the task of delivering a brief summarizing talk. Alternatively, instead of asking one person to summarize for the whole team, for a class size of 20 or less, you may conclude the activity by letting each person take a turn presenting one brief concluding remark including a personal position and one or two supporting points. This will ensure that everyone has a chance to verbalize or to express his/her opinion.

Conclusion

This activity involves the use of cooperative activities such as pairs, small groups, whole class discussions, and individual presentations. As learners share their ideas, they will have the opportunity to experiment with the language used in expressing both agreement and disagreement, and will also be required to support their opinions. As a help for learners' ability to formulate and deliver their thoughts in a clear, organized manner, provision of a sheet as presented above has proved to be an effective mediating tool, and the sheet becomes the text that learners use when they speak. Encouraging the learners' habit of jotting down thoughts has the added benefit of helping learners follow the flow of discussion, and keeping learners focused and less apprehensive during the delivery process. Instead of engaging learners in what could very possibly turn into an antagonistic debate, which may lead to adversarial discourse or feelings, this activity encourages creativity, exploration, and critical evaluation of both sides of an issue. The focus is on the promotion of communicative interaction and on encouraging learners to take a stance of respect and open-mindedness in exploring ideas, uncovering differences, and comparing and contrasting various interpretations. The mini-reflection at the end of the activity encourages learners to become more critical to take greater responsibility for their own learning, and to plan a specific goal-oriented action to attain improved oral communication skills.

Handout: Useful phrases for expressing opinion

Function	Example
Expressing opinion	▪ I think/feel/(strongly) believe that…. ▪ My opinion about this topic is that…. ▪ In my opinion/view…. ▪ It seems to me that…. ▪ It may be/It has been argued that…. ▪
Contributing an additional point	▪ I have one additional thought…. ▪ There is another way to look at it…. ▪ Following up on [name]'s comments…. ▪ What you have just said reminded me of…. ▪
Emphasizing a point	▪ It seems to me that the real issue here is…. ▪ In my opinion, the main problem at issue is…. ▪ As I see it, the most important point/key issue is…. ▪
To express agreement	▪ I (quite) agree. ▪ I (totally/completely) agree with you. ▪ That's (exactly) what I was thinking. ▪ I know what you mean. ▪ I think so, too. ▪ You are (absolutely) right. ▪ I couldn't agree with you more. ▪

Function	Example
To express disagreement	<ul><li>I disagree (with you) because…./I don't agree with you because….</li><li>I'm not sure that I (entirely) agree with you. The reason is that….</li><li>I don't think that…, because….</li><li>I think your idea is possible, but the evidence suggests/supports the interpretation that….</li><li>Are you sure? I thought…/I was under the impression that…/I would argue that….</li><li></li></ul>
Partial agreement, doubt, or reservation	<ul><li>Yes, but….</li><li>I agree with you to a certain extent, but….</li><li>I (can) see your point, but….</li><li>I see what you mean, but….</li><li>Yes, that may be true/you may be right, but….</li><li>I understand where you are coming from, but….</li><li>I agree with many of the things you have said, but….</li><li></li></ul>
Asking for clarification/elaboration	<ul><li>If I understand you correctly, you mean/this means/it means that….</li><li>I'm not sure what you mean. Do you mean…?</li><li>You mentioned (earlier) that… Do you mean…?</li><li>What do you mean (by…)?/ Could you explain what you mean by…?</li><li>So what you are saying is that….</li><li>Let me just make sure -- your point is that [paraphrase]. Is that correct?</li><li></li></ul>

Activity 3: *Informal debate -- Take 2*(For classroom instruction)

Now that you are more familiar with the mechanics and strategies introduced in Units 3 and 4, use this activity as an opportunity to build your confidence about engaging in academic discussion.

Instructions: Randomly divide the class into two groups, and have someone volunteer to be the observer for each group.

Take a look at the following topics. Work in groups to show that you are aware of both sides of a position by brainstorming the reasons (i.e., supporting statements) for those positions. Share your personal opinion with regard to both sides of the issue in question with the group and provide the reason(s). Be sure to practice, using the phrases from Units 3 and 4 for giving, eliciting, and expressing opinions.

Topic A:

Advances in technology have benefitted society.
Advances in technology have caused problems for society

Topic B:

There are advantages for international graduate students in the role of teaching/research assistant.
There are disadvantages for international graduate students in the role of teaching/research assistant.

Other topics:

_____

_____

Observer's notes:

_____

_____

_____

_____

Notes to observers: Be observant of the nature of your group's contributions by reflecting on such questions as: Is there a balanced interaction among the participants? Do some tend to speak up too early or too late? Do some speak too much or too little? Do some tend to make very lengthy comments or comments that are too brief? What sorts of questions are posed? Are they relevant? Are certain types of comment often made? Do participants challenge each other with their comments in a constructive way?

(Notes 4 and 5)

4.5 Strategies for Success

A. Turn-taking management

Monitoring to self-diagnose: In everyday conversations or group discussions, it is normal to have some interruptions. It's also common for people to begin a comment just as another speaker is finishing his/her thought. However, if you find that your talk is often being interrupted and, as a result, you don't have the time needed to finish your thoughts or ideas, consider whether any of the following issues are contributing to the problem.

☐ Does my speaking style make people want to talk more than listen? Am I being precise and concise?

☐ Have I signalled explicitly and clearly when I have finished and when I have not?

☐ Is the pause between my thoughts too long?

☐ Have I misperceived normal overlap as an interruption and not realized that I can still keep talking? In other words, have I yielded the floor too easily?

☐ Could it be the case that I got my listeners so involved that sometimes people could not hold in their reactions?

☐ Is there a pattern of interaction that might be related to power dynamics and/or gender differences in communication?

Strategies for managing interruptions: If any of the above factors might be at play in the occurrence of frequent interruptions, here are some suggestions for taking control of your turn to speak:

1. Observe the pattern of interruptions. Experiment with talking through what you *perceive* as an interruption.

2. Be aware of your own and the other person's body language, style, and pace, e.g., dropping the pitch at the end of the last sentence to signal yielding. Sending explicit verbal, vocal, and nonverbal signals to the other person may give you more control of the conversation.

3. If you pause for more than five seconds in the middle of your turn, people may assume that you have finished what you wanted to say. If you are still talking, send out explicit verbal signals(e.g., *I'm just about to finish my point.*) to let others know.

4. If you find yourself having trouble knowing when to jump into a discussion, wait for a natural break or for turn-yielding cues in the conversation. Then jump right in by starting with one of the expressions provided in this unit (e.g., *Can I make a quick comment about that?*).

5. If you notice that a person keeps on interrupting because of aggressiveness, a need for dominance, or a lack of respect, and not because of great enthusiasm or passion about the issues under discussion, then send out explicit verbal, vocal, and nonverbal turn-maintaining signals to let him/her know that you wish to maintain your turn and finish your comments.

B. Strategies and pointers for productively engaging in discussions:

☐ Concentrate on reasons, not positions. When you have a difference of opinion, find out the reasons for the differences. Listen in order to understand the thinking behind your interlocutor's reasoning. As Steven Covey (1989, 2004) once said: "Seek first to understand, then to be understood."

☐ Do your homework. The key to effective discussion is preparation. Be sure to articulate your own list of issues, questions, and answers so that you can contribute to the discussion productively.

☐ Jot down keywords. Write down a keyword or phrase from the previous person's statement to help jog your memory. Link your argument by "echoing" that part of the statement as a support to you in elaborating your argument/viewpoint.

☐ Slow down. Don't respond to pressure or urgency by making snap comments. Give yourself a few seconds to consider the question/statement and your response.

☐ Acknowledge contributions made, challenge differences in viewpoints respectfully, and respect others' viewpoints. You must recognize that the way another person perceives an issue or the approach another person takes to examine an issue may differ from your own. Listen attentively to each point or objection, acknowledge a contribution if it is helpful, respect differences of opinion, and challenge each other's thinking respectfully.

☐ Empathize. Put yourself in your conversational partner's position. Commit yourself to understanding (not necessarily agreeing with) your conversational partner's viewpoint.

☐ Though the degree of direct eye contact may vary across cultures, it's important to recognize your own preferences and those of your listener's culture. Eye contact helps your persuasiveness and ability to engage your listener, whether there is one listener or many. Looking someone in the eye directly, without staring, conveys sincerity and respect.

☐ Don't be overly ambitious. Make no more than three points, and be brief in making your points. Give your position, key supporting points, and a summary.

☐ Help your peers clarify their points and broaden their thinking and understanding of various key issues under discussion. This effort often in turn contributes to clarifying your own thinking and understanding.

☐ The quality of your participation in a discussion cannot be directly measured by the frequency of your contributions or the length of your remarks. Be critical of the nature of your contributions by reflecting on such questions as: Do you have a tendency to speak up too early or too late? Do you speak too much or too little? Do you tend to make very lengthy comments or overly brief ones? Do you tend to make certain types of comments? Do your comments challenge others in a constructive way? Do you ask relevant questions and offer helpful follow-up responses to help keep the flow of discussion on track?

☐ Practice, practice, practice. With practice comes confidence!

(Notes 6 and 7)

C. Tests of evidence to consider: Evaluate the following criteria in your own as well as others' evidence to practice strengthening your arguments and claims.

☐ **Reliability**: Is/Was the evidence drawn from sources that have been validated many times in the past?

☐ **Credibility**: Is/Was the evidence in the relevant information drawn from credible sources or authorities?

☐ **Objectivity**: Is/Was the evidence taken from sources that hold a fair and undistorted view on a question or issue?

☐ **Consistency**: Does/Did the evidence agree with other sources and is it internally consistent.

☐ **Recency**: Does/Did the evidence take into account of the most current information available?

☐ **Relevance**: Are/Were the facts and evidence presented relevant to the argument that is made?

☐ **Accuracy**: Is/Was the evidence not missing words or sources for the purpose of making it more favourable to the arguer's claim?

UNIT 5

GIVING DEPARTMENTAL PRESENTATIONS

5.1 Unit Introduction

During my years of teaching academic conversation and academic presentation skills to English-as-an-additional-language learners, I have learned that managing questions and answers that require engagement in impromptu dialogues is the task that presents the most challenges to graduate students. Even the most well-prepared students often suddenly and notably change their body language, confidence, and delivery in ways that undermine their authority during the very crucial final moments of a presentation.

Books and guides that deal with the nuts and bolts of preparing and presenting prepared monologues abound, and suggestions for those who seek them are also offered in the Appendix of this book. Unit 5, instead, focuses mainly on developing the ability to manage questions and answers in departmental presentations that involve common activities, such as making class presentations and defending proposals or theses. In these situations, questions are usually more predictable because you are often dealing with an audience known to you in a somewhat controlled situation.

This unit covers the first seven essential challenging question-and-answer situations that are commonly encountered in departmental speaking contexts. The content in this unit is designed to help you build the confidence and skills needed to field an audience's questions before moving on to dealing with an audience that may be unknown to you and in a more unpredictable situation, such as conference presentations or job talks (see Unit 7). Through diagnostic questions and application activities that are designed to develop your linguistics skills, expand your strategic repertoires, and explore your cultural awareness, the unit provides specific guidance about how to deal more confidently with questions that you may encounter at your next speaking event.

5.2 Facing Challenges and Exploring Hidden Assumptions

Diagnostic questions: Explore these questions on your own if you are using this book for self-study. In a classroom, share your thoughts about these questions with a speaking partner and be prepared to share your discussion with the class.

1. Consider the various cross-cultural dimensions that you have explored in previous units, for example, small-large power distance, high-low tolerance of ambiguity, and feminine-masculine dominated cultures. How might these dimensions affect how one approaches presenting and answering questions in academic settings?

(Note 1)

2. Share with your group how you assess yourself in terms of your personal/cultural beliefs/expectations that influence your approach/pattern in presenting and answering questions in departmental presentations? Provide personal experiences or examples.

3. What are some personal difficulties that you face or anticipate facing in fielding questions during departmental presentations (e.g., giving progress reports, making class presentations, defending proposals/theses)?

(Note 2)

4. **Fielding questions:** Explore with your speaking partner(s) some strategies that you can use to handle the following types of questions that you are likely to encounter during the question-and-answer sessions that occur in departmental presentations. Be sure to consider both the *strategies* (i.e., how would you deal with the situation?) and *language* (i.e., what would you say exactly?) that you can employ when handling each of the following situations. Work in pairs and write down what you would say for each situation.

Note: It's important that you make the effort to write down what you would say so that you have the basis for noticing the gap between your linguistic choices and the linguistic choices of your peers or your instructors that may be more effective in specific situations.

Situation 1: A "you-will-cover-later" question

What would you do?

What would you say?

Situation 2: An "off-the-subject" question

What would you do?

What would you say?

Situation 3: A "stupid" question

What would you do?

What would you say?

Situation 4: A limited-interest question

What would you do?

What would you say?

Situation 5: A rambling or long-winded question

What would you do?

What would you say?

Situation 6: A multi-question question

What would you do?

What would you say?

Situation 7: A "don't understand" or "need-more-time-to-think" question

What would you do?

What would you say?

Other: What are some other challenges identified in question 3? Together, brainstorm some strategies to help you overcome them.

5.3 Mastering the Mechanics of Language

(A) The basics of presentation lingo
Here are useful expressions that you can use in various key parts of your oral presentation. Pay attention to the language that other experienced presenters use and continue adding to the list or modifying your language.

To welcome your audience:

Good afternoon, ladies and gentlemen.   Good afternoon, everyone.
Good morning, and welcome to my presentation on....   How's everyone today?

Try adding some of your own expressions:

_____

To warm up an audience:

[Conduct a poll] How many of you have ever...?   I'd like to start by....
I'll begin by....

Try adding some of your own expressions:

_____

To introduce the subject/topic:

I'm pleased to be here today to talk to you about....   The purpose of my presentation is....
Today, I'm going to talk about my recent/current research on....   The topic of my presentation is....
Thank you for this opportunity to share with you my research on....
Thank you for your (kind) introduction. As X just explained, I am here to talk to you about....

Try adding some of your own expressions:

_____

To explain the division of material:

Time does not allow me to cover all aspects of my research in 20 minutes, so I intend to focus on....
In today's talk, I plan to examine/cover the following three issues: 1..., 2..., and 3....
...I hope to provide answers to three questions that people often ask about....Those questions are as follows....

Try adding some of your own expressions:

_____

To give instructions about asking and answering questions:

Do feel free to interrupt me if you have any questions.
I'll try to answer all of your questions *after* the presentation.
Please save your questions until the end of my presentation.

Try adding some of your own expressions:

_____

To provide a note of finality:

To conclude..../In conclusion....　　　　　　　　　　Now, to sum up....
Now, I'd like to recap.../close by....　　　　　　　　Finally..../In closing....
Before opening the floor to questions, let me briefly summarize what I have covered.
Let's summarize briefly what we've looked at/covered/considered....
We've considered/examined the three points... (A, B, and C). In the future, we may want to consider (E) and (F).
That brings me to the end of my presentation.

Try adding some of your own expressions:

_____

_____

To thank your audience:

Thank you (for your courteous attention).
Thank you very much for your input/questions this morning/afternoon.

Try adding some of your own expressions:

_____

_____

To invite questions:

Now, I'll try to answer any questions that you may have.
Now, I'd be pleased to answer any questions that you may have.
Are there any questions?

Try adding some of your own expressions:

_____

_____

To signal transitions between sections:

Next, let's move on to....　　　　　　　　　　　　Turning now to....
Now, I'd like to shift our attention to....　　　　　　The first issue leads us to the second issue about....
So far, we have discussed.... Next, I want to focus on....
So far, we have considered... Now, I'd like to draw your attention to....
Now that we understand X, let us begin to consider Y.
Before moving on to the next category, let me give one more example.
Let's go on to the next aspect/characteristic of....
So that explains the procedure, but what benefits does it have?

Try adding some of your own expressions:

_____

_____

To use rhetorical questions as transitional devices:

Where does this leave us?　　　　　　　　　　　　Where do we go from here?
What can we expect from this?

Try adding some of your own expressions:

_____

_____

To emphasize points:

The main thing is....

It's important to emphasize at this point that....

The key point is....

This is the most crucial step in the process....

Try adding some of your own expressions:

(B) Communication strategies and language for fielding questions Here are some suggested strategies and language for fielding the first seven challenging situations covered in this unit. If you feel competent to deal with the situations covered in this unit and wish to move on to other challenging situations, you can skip to Unit 7.

1. A "you-will-cover-later" question

- If it's a question that you can answer briefly right away, do so. For example: "The short answer to your question is 'yes,' and I will be addressing your question fully when I get to the Methodology section, which is coming up next."

- Be *specific* about when you will be addressing a listener's question if you choose to postpone answering it so that the question does not disrupt the flow of your presentation. For example: "Thank you for raising the point about... I have considered that issue, and I will be covering it in the Discussion section of my presentation. Please ask your question again if that section does not provide clarity for you."

- You also might like to remind the questioner when you get to that section: "This is related to the question you raised earlier..."

2. An "off-the-subject" question

- If it's a question that you can answer quickly, always comment on it *very briefly*.

- If a question is off the subject and would move the focus away from your talk, consider postponing it until the end of your presentation. For example: "That's an interesting question, but it seems to be more related to... Would you mind if we discuss it after the presentation?"

- Note that sometimes a seemingly irrelevant or off-the-subject question may not be so. It could very well be a questioner's indirect way of getting to the heart of the question that he/she has in mind. If you are unsure about the question's relevance, check with the person who raised the question by politely asking "How does the question relate to the topic at hand? The question seems to be more related to...."

3. A "stupid" question

- First, there is really no "stupid" question. Some questions that are seemingly simple on the surface might lead to stimulating discussion about your work. Consider each question as an opportunity for you to clarify your work or to emphasize the key points that you intend to convey to your audience members. Be tactful, and never insult the questioner! If it's a question that answered already: "This is the same question that [name] raised earlier. Let me answer it again briefly. This is an important question. Let me approach/answer this issue in a different way."

4. A limited-interest question

- For comments that you can comment on very briefly, your priority is always to answer your audience's questions. For questions that seem obscure or of limited interest, and that might take valuable time away from the focus of your presentation, then, as with the strategy recommended for dealing with an "off-the-subject" question, postpone the question and discuss it with the questioner one-on-one after your presentation. Having said that, you need to make sure that the question is indeed a "limited interest" question by using the following approach:

"Thank you for your question. The question you have raised is a complicated one that merits more time to answer fully. How many of you would like to spend some time discussing this question?"

If only one person raises his/her hand, then it's safe to table the question until after the presentation: "Would you mind if I address your question if we have some time left at the end of the question-and-answer session, or else when the formal presentation has ended?" If several people raise their hands, then perhaps the question is not of limited interest and deserves some time during the question-and-answer session.

5. A rambling or long-winded question

- Many international graduate students find this communication style very challenging to face in either a seminar discussion or a question-and-answer session. Many students are quick to share their experiences of feeling panic about not knowing whether one has missed the question as the questioner's monologue continues, and at the same time feeling too embarrassed to ask the questioner to repeat something he/she said a while earlier. Does this sound familiar? The key is to interrupt as soon as you find yourself getting lost in a question that lacks focus or not understanding what the question means. For example:

    "Excuse me for interrupting… so the question you are asking is..." (with rising intonation).
    "Excuse me for interrupting… so what you need to know from me is..." (with rising intonation).

  Avoid waiting until the end or asking, "Could you repeat your question?"!

6. A multi-question question

- Another situation that intimidates many international graduate students is facing multiple questions at once or a question that includes multiple sub-questions. Zero in on one point/question at a time. For example: "You've raised a lot of important issues. Let me try to respond. On the matter of…"

- If time is very limited, prompt the questioner to choose the question that he/she would like you to answer. For example: "Those are important issues, but I don't think we have enough time to address them all. What is the main question that you would like me to answer?"

- If you do not feel comfortable answering multiple questions at once, try interrupting politely as soon as the questioner starts moving on to the second part of a question by saying, for example: "Before you move on to the next question, may I answer your first question first?"

- If you feel comfortable dealing with multiple questions, consider jotting down a key word or two to remind you of the questions raised so that you can state the focus of each question to remind the audience before you answer it. In this way, you will also avoid repeating: "What was your second question again?" "What was your third question again?" You may say, instead: "To answer your first question… On the question about… Finally, your question concerning…."

7. A "don't understand" or "need-more-time-to-think" question

- Ask for repetition, clarification, or elaboration when you are not certain if you have understood the question (Review Unit 3). For example: "Would you mind repeating the question so that I can be sure I understand you?"

- If you need a few moments to think about the question and/or to formulate a response, send explicit verbal signals to let your listener know. For example: "That's an excellent question. Let me think about it for a few moments."

- If it's a question that you think you can answer, but you need more than a few moments to flesh out your ideas, postpone it. For example: That's an excellent question that I need more time to consider. Can we come back to this question later?"

- Also, use visual aids (e.g., the blackboard, whiteboard, flipchart available onsite) to help you answer a question when you need more time to formulate a well-thought-out response, and your response can be presented visually.

5.4   Application Activities

Activity 1: *Panel activity for experts and questioners*(For classroom instruction)

Instructions: This extends the panel discussion activity introduced in Unit 3. Assign another short article that has current relevance to the academic community or a short research article of public interest that students from various disciplines can understand and discuss. This time, randomly divide the class into two groups, one expert group and one questioner group, or reverse the role that each individual played the last time, for the purpose of practicing fielding questions.

Preparation Period (20 minutes):

Expert Group: Read the article and anticipate questions that the Questioner Group might raise. Group members might consider designating different members to be responsible for responding to certain aspects of the article (e.g., the methodology, findings, interpretation, recommendations, and so on). By doing so, the group can ensure that there is a balance in participation and contributions among members and members can practice refining how those anticipated questions will be answered.

Questioner Group: Randomly assign individuals to be responsible for generating questions that correspond to each of the six challenging situations. During the process of generating challenging questions, keep in mind the content that you learned and practiced in Unit 3 about asking questions.

Question Period (30 minutes): Start the 10-mimute question period much like any question-and-answer session after a departmental presentation. Once the question period is complete, both the Expert and Questioner Groups will reflect on their performance and share their reflections about challenges, discoveries, or successes with the class. Reverse the role that each individual plays so that participants can practice both asking and responding to questions, and reflect on their challenges and successes after carrying out the activity.

Reflection 1 (Role: Expert):

Reflection 2 (Role: Questioner):

Activity 2: *Self-assessment*

For self-study or a take-home task: Video-tape yourself or have someone video-tape you delivering a 10-minute talk describing your research project. Complete the worksheet, and share it with a family member, friend, or colleague who would be interested in offering you feedback.

For classroom instruction: Video-tape each student practicing the delivery of a 5- to 10-minute talk in class. The talk is a description of his/her research project or of a few key concepts in the student's field. Ask the student to complete the following self-assessment sheet for the next class or to share their discoveries with his or her peers in class.

Self-assessment Worksheet

Try viewing the tape at least three times, **each time focusing on a different aspect of your speaking** (e.g., your body language, vocal image, and verbal image). Answer the following questions before moving on to the next section.

1.   What, if anything, surprised you as you watched your presentation clip?

2.   What did you notice about your non-verbal language? What aspect(s) of your ***non-verbal image*** would you like to improve?

(Note 3)

3.   What did you notice about the vocal qualities of your talk? What aspect(s) of your ***vocal image*** would you like to improve?

4.   Comment on ***the use of language*** in your talk. What have you noticed? What aspect(s) would you like to improve?

5.   Comment on the ***structure and content*** of your talk. What would you like to change or improve?

6.   Overall, what do you like about your talk? Please identify ***three or more strengths*** you noticed from watching the clip.

(Note 4)

5.5 Strategies for Success

A. Tips on successfully handling audience questions:
First, consider every question an *opportunity* to clarify or emphasize your key points, to strengthen your ideas, and to convey your passion about your area of expertise! Here are some strategies to keep in mind for answering questions professionally. These strategies apply not only to departmental presentations, but are also highly applicable and relevant to presentations in other academic venues.

1. **Preparation, preparation, preparation.** Anticipate questions that may come up. In the process of trying to answer some (or all) of your questions, you will gain knowledge. You will increase your self-confidence in responding to both expected and unexpected questions.

2. **Listen** carefully to the *entire* question BEFORE you begin to answer it.

3. **Pause.** Think before responding. Use visual aids (e.g., blackboard, whiteboard, or flipchart) to help you answer the question.

4. **Repeat or paraphrase the question.** This serves several purposes:

   - For a large audience, this ensures that the entire audience hears the question. It's important that everyone hears the question; otherwise, the answer you provide may not make sense to those who didn't catch what has been asked.
   - It lets you check your understanding of the question. When you have not completely understood the question, the person asking often will rephrase or elaborate further upon the question.
   - If you have understood the question, it will allow you some additional time to evaluate the question and to formulate a response.
   - This also gives everyone time to think about the question and possibly respond to it.

5. Paraphrase **negative** questions. Don't repeat a negative question, paraphrase. For example: "So your question concerns the fundamental postulate and self-reporting method used for my research. Let me clarify them...."

6. **You may ask your own question** for elaboration. For example: *Could you provide an example? Could you provide the context?*

7. **Ask the questioner about his/her thoughts/perspective.** As we all know, we often have an idea/position about the question before we ask it.

8. **Answer directly and honestly.** Answer the question as best as you can. Your answer should be *concise (brief) and precise (to the point).*

9. Be aware of your **nonverbal language** (e.g., show you are listening by nodding and making eye contact).

10. After responding, you may want to **check** to see if you have really answered the question by saying something like the following: *Does that answer your question? Was that what you were asking? Is that the kind of information you were seeking?*

11. If **after two or three attempts** you still have not answered the question to the questioner's satisfaction, and others can't seem to help answer it, then suggest getting together after your presentation. For example: *I suggest that we get together after the presentation, and we can talk more specifically about this.*

12. **Have a pen and paper available.** Jot down key words, phrases, or questions that you cannot answer. Promise to get back to the person and do get back to him/her.

13. **Involve the whole audience.** This can be done through eye contact with the entire audience while you are answering questions, and not just speaking to the questioner the entire time.

14. **Maintain the same delivery style.** Avoid having two distinct delivery styles: one poised and confident (i.e., the portion of your talk that you were able to rehearse) and one distinctively lacking confidence (i.e., the question-and-answer session where you are dealing with unknown audience members or unfamiliar questions).

15. **Avoid saying: "This will be our last question."** This limits your opportunity to take another question if your attempt in answering the final question was less than satisfactory. Always try to end your presentation on a positive note when possible!

(Note 5)

B. Basics of effective language use: The purpose of this unit is not to present the detailed coverage about how to craft a speech, which is the focus of many oral presentation guides. Instead, it emphasizes the basics of language use that a speaker should keep in mind when drafting a speech or answering questions. Even those who consider themselves highly competent may still want to remind themselves of the basic principles of effective language use.

1. **Accuracy.** Use words that will help your listeners to understand your meaning as precisely as possible. The immediacy of speaking makes it challenging to find the exact words you want on the spot; that is why a preparation that includes anticipating and answering potential questions is critical in maximizing the accuracy of your word choice and meaning.

2. **Simplicity.** Avoid complex sentences and needless hedging terms. Your objective is to get the audience to understand your intended message.

3. **Conciseness.** Using words efficiently and omitting unnecessary words will help you enhance the clarity of your message. Avoid taking too long to get to your point if you have a tendency to communicate in a round-about way.

4. **Coherence.** An oral presentation does not have the visible punctuation marks and written words that are in a text. Provide logical connections among your ideas to enhance understanding and retention of your message.

5. **Limit jargon, abbreviations, and acronyms**, or use them very carefully to avoid alienating listeners who may not share that language. Never assume shared understanding or make your audience guess what you mean.

6. **Define terms.** If the term has an important role in the argument, and your usage of the term departs from ordinary usage, or if there's a chance that your listeners might not understand the term in the way that you intended, then you should always define the term. These definitions help reduce unwanted connotations or ambiguities.

7. **Express your ideas vividly.** An important element of a memorable talk is the vividness of how the message is expressed. Avoid passive voice and bookish language. Instead, use active voice, everyday language, personalized constructions, and/or colourful terms that appeal to listeners' sensibilities in order to engage them.

8. **Use bias-free language.** Be aware of how certain expressions may reflect unconscious assumptions about groups that may be a part of your audience. Using such language undermines the argument's effectiveness. Avoid using gender-biased, race- and ethnicity- biased, age-biased, and disability-biased language.

9. **Organize your points strategically.** Your strongest arguments should be placed at either the beginning or the end of the message; such placement will make a greater impression and will be more memorable.

10. Keep in mind Aristotle's **three key elements of persuasiveness**, which stand the test of time: (1) *Logos*(i.e., the appeal to the audience's reason; the rational proof associated with formal logic and the citation of relevant facts and objective evidence -- statistics, case histories, surveys, facts, examples, precedents -- within the message; and the progression of the talk from point to point logically; (2) *Pathos*(i.e., the appeal to the audience's emotions); and (3) *Ethos* (i.e., the degree of confidence the audience has in the speaker on the basis of his/her character, personality, and credibility).

(Notes 6 and 7)

C. Preparing to answer questions in your proposal or thesis defense: Before you prepare for the questions and answers, covering a few points will help you to avoid some very common pitfalls.First, always review your department's proposal or thesis defense guidelines, and consult with your supervisor. Be sure to follow the guidelines and your supervisor's advice exactly during the preparation process, and follow the presentation guidelines that many speaking guides offer about how to prepare and communicate your presentation. (See Notes on the Unit section for some suggested references.) Second, never expect all committee members to remember or to have read your work thoroughly before the defense. As such, you need to present essential information in the specific time limit allocated for the presentation component of your defense in order to inform your committee members about what you did, why you did it, how you did it, and what the implications/contributions are.

Following your 15 to 20-minute thesis proposal or thesis presentation comes the stage when most candidates feel great anxiety: You will be expected to answer questions from committee members and an external examiner in a session that normally lasts one to two hours. Committee members and examiners may ask questions about any area of your thesis work. The best strategy to get ready for fielding questions during a proposal or thesis defense is no different from the method you would use to prepare for any academic oral presentation – anticipate questions and prepare answers. For example, you know where the weaknesses of your work are, so don't go to the defense without preparing to address those weaknesses.

Here are some common question types to go over when you prepare for a proposal or thesis defense:

1. Questions that seek your clarification (e.g., Could you clarify the point you made about...?)
2. Questions that probe your grasp of the technical issues (e.g., Could you explain the basis for choosing parametric over non-parametric statistical method to examine your data?)
3. Questions that ask you to explain why you took a certain approach (e.g., Why is X important to the analysis, as opposed to other frameworks for analyzing the data? Why did you choose to use X method?)
4. Questions about what would happen if something were modified (e.g., If you had to do the study all over again, what would you do differently?)
5. Questions about the limitations of your work (e.g., Discuss the methodological limitations of your research. What would you improve?)
6. Questions about future directions for your work (e.g., What recommendations do you have for future research? Is this a line of research that you intend to pursue beyond the thesis? If so, how?)
7. Questions about the main (theoretical, methodological, empirical, and practical) contributions of your work (e.g., Discuss the theoretical, methodological, and practical implications of your research. What recommendations and implications are there for practitioners in your field?)
8. Other: What are you most proud of?

It's helpful to keep in mind that most committee members are genuinely inquisitive or curious about your work; so think of the process as a dialogue with your future colleagues. It's not uncommon for them to raise questions that they themselves cannot answer, and they are interested in your thinking process and in knowing what you think, now that you are an expert in your own area. In the event that you find yourself in a potentially hostile situation, defend your work, but don't get defensive. Remember that, even though committee members are experts in their own respective fields, you know your work better than anyone on the committee. Apply the strategies for fielding questions covered in Units 5 and 7. For tips on how to overcome speech anxiety, refer to Unit 7.

UNIT 6

TEACHING IN THE CLASSROOM

6.1 Unit Introduction

Unit 6 is devoted to speaking skills in teaching settings, where graduate students' language skills and sensitivity to cultural differences are challenged by their new roles as teaching assistants. Exploring hidden assumptions from both the students' and the teachers' perspectives is critical in your efforts to develop the speaking repertoires necessary for effective communication in the classroom. The recurring key components in this unit of Facing Challenges and Exploring Hidden Assumptions, Mastering the Mechanics of Language, Application Activities, and Strategies for Success are designed to encourage you to experiment with ways to enhance your ability to communicate with students in one-on-one settings, to ask questions that tap into students' thinking at different levels, to clarify explanations, to handle students' questions, and deal with challenging teaching situations with enhanced confidence. The functional language for delivering a lecture is covered in the Mechanics of Language section in Unit 7; the mechanics can be applied in both TA situations where you need to deliver a lecture to students or at a teaching demonstration during your campus visit for an interview. The Strategies for Success section includes suggestions for bridging cultural/language gaps, vocabulary strategies to maintain fluency during speaking, and pointers in facilitating discussions that promote dialogical exchanges.

6.2 Facing Challenges and Exploring Hidden Assumptions

Diagnostic questions: Explore these questions on your own if you use this book for self-study. In a classroom, share your thoughts about these questions with a speaking partner and be prepared to share your discussion with the class.

1. Students' classroom behaviours in your country may differ from those in North America. Share your personal perceptions of what Canadian/American students are like, based on your own observations in the classroom. What surprised you the most?

(Note 1)

2. What are some of your expectations about how students and instructors should behave and learn in your culture? Share these expectations with your speaking partner(s). Do you and your speaking partner(s) share the same expectations? Try asking your English-speaking colleagues to share their expectations with you. What have you discovered? What are some strategies that you can use to bridge the cultural gap?

(Note 2)

3. How would you introduce a syllabus for a course on the first day of class?

4. How do you usually go about defining terms in your teaching? Explain how you would vary your ways of defining a term in your teaching on the basis of the following situations:

    a. You are introducing the term for the first time.
    b. The students have forgotten the term you introduced previously.
    c. The students did not understand the term.
    d. The students know the term but do not know how it is used in your field.
    e. The students mixed up the term with another term.

5. With a speaking partner, choose *one* of the following, and consider how you would give instruction to your students.

    a. How to follow lab safety procedures
    b. How to use a particular instrument for...
    c. How to calculate the results of...

6. Dealing with challenging teaching situations: Explore with your speaking partner(s) some strategies that you can use to handle the following situations that you may encounter in your teaching. Be sure to consider both the *strategies* (i.e., how would you deal with the situation?) and *language* (i.e., what would you say exactly?) that you can use when handling each of the following situations. Work in pairs and write down what you would say for each situation.

(Note 3)

Situation 1: Those who like to shake their heads negatively about whatever you or other students are saying

What would you do?

What would you say?

Situation 2: Those who are habitually late to class

What would you do?

What would you say?

Situation 3: Those who tend to ramble on and on

What would you do?

What would you say?

Situation 4: Those who tend to be very quiet

What would you do?

What would you say?

Situation 5: Those who read newspapers or books that are not relevant to your class

What would you do?

What would you say?

Situation 6: Those who like to chit-chat while you are teaching

What would you do?

What would you say?

Situation 7: Those who tend to hog the discussion

What would you do?

What would you say?

Situation 8: Those who like to argue

What would you do?

What would you say?

Situation 9: Those who believe or want others to believe that they know it all

What would you do?

What would you say?

Situation 10: Those whose performance seems to be sliding

What would you do?

What would you say?

Situation 11: Those who are not attentive in class

What would you do?

What would you say?

Situation 12: Those who like to complain about their grades

What would you do?

What would you say?

7. Together with your partner, brainstorm 2 to 3 strategies that you as an international teaching assistant can use to enhance clarity of explanations in a lecture/tutorial/lab session.

6.3 Mastering the Mechanics of Language

(A) Holding office hours   Holding office hours is one of the many usual duties that teaching assistants have. As crucial links between the course instructor and the students, teaching assistants are expected to be available for questions and to be responsive to reasonable requests that will help students learn. Office time is a means of strengthening that important link and is important because it provides opportunities for you to interact with students individually and to offer one-on-one assistance. Here are some common phrases for interactions during office hours. Try modifying the expressions provided here or adding some of your own language for these interactions.

1. **Be inviting:** TAs are often advised to keep their doors open during office hours to make it easy for students to locate their TAs and also easy for TAs to keep meetings professional. Check with the university/department's TA guidelines or consult with your supervising professor if you are uncertain about proper conduct when you meet with individual students during office hours or for coffee.

   How are you doing? Come on in. Glad you dropped by.

2. **For a meeting that is not scheduled:** Be explicit about the amount of time you have for the drop-in.

   This is a good time. I am not expecting another student for 20 minutes or so. (Note: This sends out a clear signal to the student about the time frame.)

3. **Where to sit:**

   Why don't you pull a chair over?   Please take a seat/have a seat.

4. **Setting the climate:**

   How was Monday's quiz for you?   How is your research project coming along?
   I noticed that you raised a very good question the other day...

5. **Problem solving:**

   How do you study for this course?   What do you think are the key arguments advanced by X?
   Are there other students in the course whom you know and can talk to about the course content?

6. **Offering advice:**

   You might try..../You might want to refer to....   Perhaps you might like to consider....
   I would suggest/recommend that you....   Have you ever thought of speaking to....
   Have you thought about taking a different approach?   Another thing (that) I'd recommend is....
   It (might/would) be a good idea to....   If I were you/in your shoes, I would....
   My advice would be....

7. **Clarifying unexpressed issues or concerns:**

   Is there anything else that I can help you with?   What other concerns do you have about the project?
   Have I answered all your questions today?

8. **Wrapping up:**

   If you have more questions as you review the material, feel free to drop by.
   We must wrap up in a few minutes. I am expecting another student.
   If there's anyone else outside the door, could you please ask the person to come in?
   I think we have time for one more question. (Note: When the time is almost up, let your student know.)

(B) Generating questions at different levels

Bloom (1956, 1984) is well-known for creating the taxonomy of higher level thinking questions. Use Bloom's taxonomy that puts questions in hierarchical categories of thinking skills from less complex to those that require higher order level of thinking as a starting point for practice in generating questions.

Levels	Key verbs for generating questions
Facts/Knowledge	tell, list, describe, define, identify, show, label, quote, name, who, when, and where.
Comprehension	summarize, describe, report, outline, interpret, contrast, predict, associate, discuss, and restate
Application	apply, demonstrate, construct, illustrate, show, solve, modify, relate, change, classify, and experiment
Analysis	analyze, distinguish, examine, explain, connect, classify, divide, compare, contrast, explain, and infer
Synthesis	combine, integrate, modify, substitute, create, design, invent, compose, formulate, and generalize
Evaluation	assess, justify, decide, argue, test, rate, measure, recommend, convince, select, and support

(Note 4)

(C) Handling students' questions

In teaching situations, handling students' questions involves your ability to provide your students information that they need. For that purpose, it's important to enhance your ability to spontaneously use the various strategies that are available to accomplish that task, such as restating a question to make sure that you have understood it or to create some time for you to formulate your response. In addition, handling students' questions for teaching purposes also involves your ability to provide appropriate follow-up statements or questions that serve various teaching functions, such as making sure that everyone has heard the question in order to engage everyone in the process, modifying the question to channel students' thinking or attention, acknowledging and encouraging students' input in order to motivate their participation, and making your answer more concise for material that you have covered before or will be covering later.

1. *Restating* questions for specific purposes:

a. To make sure that everyone heard the question:

Did everyone hear that? X's question was….   That's a good question. X wants to know…
I want to make sure that everyone heard you. Would you repeat your question?
Student: What is the lab assignment for this week?   TA: X's question is what the lab assignment is for this week.

Try adding some of your own expressions:

b. To give yourself time to think:

Yes. I see what you are asking. You want to know.... Let me think....
Your question is.... That's a very interesting question. I need to think for a bit before I answer.
So you want to know.... I don't know the answer to that question, but I will try to find out by the next class.

Try adding some of your own expressions:

_____

_____

c. If you are 100% certain that you understand the question:

Your question is....   What you are asking is....
X's question is....   X wants to know....
X is asking....   What you are asking is....

Student: Can we hand in our assignments tomorrow?
TA: You would like to know whether you can hand in your assignments tomorrow.

Student: How long do we have to do the assignment?
TA: You would like to know how long you have to do the assignment.

Try adding some of your own expressions:

_____

_____

d. If you are unsure of what the question was:

Do you mean...?   If I understand you correctly....
If I am not mistaken, you'd like to know....   I think what you want to know is.... Am I right?

Try adding some of your own expressions:

_____

_____

e. If you did not understand the question at all:

Would you repeat your question, please? I didn't quite catch what you said.

Try adding some of your own expressions:

_____

_____

f. To modify the question:

Student: What's the difference between the midterm and the final?
TA: Do you mean relative weight, types of questions...?

Let me ask that question another way....
In this course we don't need to worry about that, but what we do want to know is....
In this course we don't need to worry about that, but the question that we need to ask ourselves is....

Try adding some of your own expressions:

_____

_____

2. To make your answers concise:

The simple answer is..., but let me explain it in a little more detail.
That's a complicated issue, but, in simple terms... We'll be covering that issue in great detail when we get to Chapter X.
Your question reminded everyone about what we covered two weeks ago when we talked about... If you recall....

Try adding some of your own expressions:

---

3. To encourage questions:

Can anyone tell me what theorem we should use to solve this problem?
What do the rest of you think?   Can anyone tell me why?
Could you say a bit more about that?   Would you elaborate on that?
Could someone give another example of...?   Would someone like to add to that?

Try adding some of your own expressions:

---

4. To recognize students input:

X is rightly reminding us of a point of view that we have neglected.
Thanks, X, for pointing that out.   Excellent point! Let's look at the issue X raised.

Try adding some of your own expressions:

---

5. Responses to correct answers:

You've got it!   Exactly/Precisely!
That's precisely it!   Right on the mark.
Did everyone hear what X just said?

Try adding some of your own expressions:

---

6. Responses to incorrect answers:

That's a very good guess, but that's not it.   Nice try, but that's not it.
Do the rest of you agree?   What do the rest of you think?

Try adding some of your own expressions:

(Note: If possible, avoid providing the correct answer right away. Consider how you can involve the entire class in the question-and-answer, so that instead of doing all the answering yourself, you create learning opportunities for your students. Try asking different types or levels of questions based on what you have heard to facilitate depth of processing/critical thinking by your students. For strategies for handing challenging questions, refer to Units 5 and 7.)

(D)Enhancing the clarity of explanations

Clarity in presenting explanations is a key attribute of an instructor's effectiveness in communicating ideas, concepts, theories, and so on. Your ability to explain things in a clear and unambiguous way is critical to creating a productive learning experience for students. Researchers have established the effectiveness of various instructional techniques, such as the use of concrete examples to illustrate abstract concepts, the use of analogies from outside of classroom, the creation of context, and so on (e.g., Tobin & Fraser, 1990;van Rooyen, 1994). Here are eight key techniques to get you started on developing the ability to achieve your communication goals.

a. Provide a definition: Provide a formal definition for the term you are teaching. Then you can supplement it with additional information (e.g., life experiences, practical applications) to make your explanation clear, memorable, and relevant to your students.

For example: The term X is defined (by [name]) as.... It is important because....
The dictionary defines the term X as....
X (the term you are defining) is a type of Y (the category to which it belongs) that is related to Z, but differs from Z in (the differentiation of the item from other relevant members)....

Your example:

b. Use a practical example: Give an example from the students' experience.

For example: To understand what X is, think of....

Your example:

c. Share a personal experience: Give an example from your experience (a story or event).

For example: To help you understand what X is, let me share a personal experience/let me give you an example.... This is called X, which means....

Your example:

d. Use an analogy: Make an analogy to some other concept that students already know. Think in terms of, for example, patterns, relationships, or functions similar to the concept that you are teaching.

For example: The structure of X is like that of the Y... The same way that....
The concept of X is analogous to....

Your example:

e. Offer comparison and contrast: Compare the term with a similar term or contrast it with an opposing term.

For example: X is similar to Y because…, but is different from Y because….

Your example:

f. Refer to word origin: Tell your students the origin of the term.

For example: The term X comes from the word Y, which means….
X is an acronym that stands for….
Use prefix or suffix: Prefix comes from Latin. It has two parts: "pre," which means "before" and "fix" from "fixus," which means "to attach"….
Atherosclerosis comes from the Greek words "athero" (meaning "paste") and "sclerosis" (meaning hardness"). It refers to the process/condition in which….

Your example:

g. Link to previously learned material: Tie together the concept/term to previously learned material or what students know already.

For example: The concept X is related to what we discussed/learned about…last week.

Your example:

h. Provide visual means: Provide a visual illustration of the term/concept (picture, drawing, diagram, or chart)

For example: This chart shows the relationship between….
This diagram will help you understand….

Your example:

(Note 5)

Now that you have a firm grasp of the eight techniques for enhancing the clarity of explanations, keep in mind such points as projecting your voice and enunciating words clearly, structuring the content logically, using verbal signals to provide a context (e.g., There are three basic principles of X. Let's look at the first one in detail…) and to emphasize a point (e.g., It's important to emphasize at this point…), providing transitions to guide your students' listening (refer to Section 6.3, To signal transitions between sections), repeating key information by saying it in different ways or repeating key words, communicating with nonverbal language, and asking questions that contribute to ensuring that your explanations are clear to students.

It's important to point out that the eight techniques presented here contribute to creating context, which is a key to effective teaching and learning. Mastering such communication involves much more, however, than simply adding pieces of information to teaching events. The context that you create with those techniques must take account of students' cognitive perceptions in relation to several levels of information, such as the connection between the current learning content and other aspects within the same content (i.e., the micro-context), its relation with other contents in the curriculum (i.e., the meso-context), and its relation with the reality of the living world outside the classroom (i.e., the macro-context).

(E) Dealing with challenging teaching situations
Before dealing with some of the challenging situations presented here, it's important to keep in mind that most students will appreciate your efforts to reach out to them and to show that you care about their learning. A general good principle to follow in communicating with students in those situations is to focus on the issue and to not take the comments or behaviours personally. Suspend personal judgements or assumptions, and address the issue with seriousness, clarity, respect, and firmness. Use the following strategies as a starting point as you fine-tune your communication with individual students.

Situation 1: The head shaker

- It's difficult to ignore someone who shakes his/her head negatively about what you or other students are saying halfway through the turn. Try focusing on the student who is speaking or on finishing up your point; then acknowledge the disagreement.
- You may respond, for example: "Andrew, I see you are shaking your head. It looks like you disagree with what is being said. Would you like to share your reactions with the rest of the class?" "Let's make the decision after weighing on all the suggestions and alternatives." "You may be right, but we are tackling the problem as a group in order to come up with new solutions. Let's see if we can gain new insights and learn new ways of looking at the problem from each other."

Other strategies?

Situation 2: The habitual latecomer

- Always start on time regardless of whether all students are there.
- In response to latecomers' repeated requests for your notes: "Do you know anyone else in the class from whom you can get notes? After that, if you have further questions, come to see me during my office hours, and we can talk about those questions specifically."

Other strategies?

Situation 3: The rambler

- If the student digresses or his/her talk is veering off track, bring everyone back on track.
- For example: "Let's focus on the question/the topic ... at hand...."

Other strategies?

Situation 4: The quiet type

- Be sensitive to students' different participation styles. Silence may be a sign of deference in certain cultures rather than a sign of passivity, lack of interest, shyness, or lack of engagement in the classroom. Use "warm" calls to invite those who tend to be quieter to contribute by saying, for example: "X, would you be willing to share your personal thoughts after we have heard from X?"
- Provide acknowledgement or encouragement: "Thanks for making the point about..../asking the question about...." "That was an excellent point you made. I hope we will continue to hear your thoughts in class."

Other strategies?

Situation 5: The newspaper reader

- Be firm and direct. "X, this is not the time to read the paper. Is there something relevant to our class discussion that you'd like to share? If not, could you please do that after class? Thank you."

Other strategies?

Situation 6: The chit-chatter

- "It makes it hard for the members of the class to hear each other when you two are talking. Could you please save it for after class?"

Other strategies?

Situation 7: The discussion hog

- X, I'll come back to you shortly. Let's see if someone else wants to grab the floor or has something to say for a minute." "Let's see if someone has a different take on this."

Other strategies?

Situation 8: The debater

- Be mindful of students' tolerance for ambiguity. Some may have a lower tolerance for ideas and propositions that run counter to their own belief systems or structures of knowledge. It's also important to recognize that when students express viewpoints that are contrary to yours, their statements are not necessarily challenges to your authority. Communicate in a way that guides them toward thinking about other perspectives. For example: "What do you see as the alternatives?" "How do you think the author could strengthen his argument?" "Let's examine some of the reasons why there is real debate about the issue." "Let's take a look at the issue from a different perspective."

Other strategies?

Situation 9: The know-it-all

- These are students who believe that they know everything or want others to perceive them as such. In addition to hogging every opportunity to answer questions, they may try to answer questions that are addressed to you or may even contradict your explanations or the information you have provided, to the point of undermining your authority as a teaching assistant. Reassert the primacy of your authority by stating the importance of looking at different perspectives on the issue and of pointing out areas that might have been overlooked. Refocus students' attention on the explanation you have provided.

- For example: "What do you think about the argument made by X in his/her most recent work?" "Although there may be some disagreement among researchers in the field about how to define X, there is a growing consensus about the key elements of what constitutes X, as presented in the definition I provided you."

Other strategies?

Situation 10: Sliding

- "I've noticed that you are missing classes lately and that you did not submit your last assignment. Is everything alright?"
- If the student's problem is beyond your capacity and duties as a teaching assistant, refer the student to other support services (e.g., counselling services) on campus.

Other strategies?

Situation 11: The inattentive student

- Assign the student as the team facilitator for a group discussion or task.
- "X, the rest of your group looks busy. Could you please find out from the group what you can do to contribute?"

Other strategies?

Situation 12: The grade complainer

- Resist the temptation to respond on the spot if the issue requires another close look. For example:

I'd like to take some time to reconsider your grade on that question.
I'd like to take a look at your answer again, and then make my final decision. I will make clear the basis for my decision. If you still don't agree with the grade, then I would encourage you to speak to Professor X.

- When you are ready to meet with the student, be prepared, clarify the grading criteria provided by your supervising professor, and cite reasons and examples to support your decision.
- When dealing with any complaints, always maintain a united front with your supervising professor, and never criticize the professor in front of students.

Other strategies?

Other: Are there other challenging situations that you have encountered in your teaching or have identified in Section 6.2 (question 6)?

6.4 Application Activities

Activity 1: *Course introduction*(For classroom instruction)

Work with a partner to prepare your mini-demo. Each of you will present one part of the introduction based on the number (1 or 2) you are assigned. Please feel free to give each other feedback during the preparation process and on the presentation.

For Student 1:

1. Opening:

2. Self-introduction:

3. Course Information:

4. Topics:

For Student 2:

1. Course requirements:

2. Grading policy:

3. Closing:

Activity 2: *Micro-teaching exercise*

For self-study or a take-home task: Choose to apply one or more of the strategies from the "Enhancing the clarity of explanations" section, and prepare the language that you will use to communicate key concepts, theories, or ideas in your teaching for seven consecutive sessions. Reflect on what worked and what did not work for each application. What are your observations about students' comprehension of your explanations over time? Are there certain strategies to which students respond most positively? Continue to apply those strategies in your teaching so that they can become part of your teaching repertoire.

For classroom instruction: Assign students to prepare a 10-minute micro-teaching session with content related to what they will be doing in their own teaching contexts. Students must apply the strategies from the "Enhancing the clarity of explanations" section in their delivery in class. Video-tape or audio-tape each student practicing the delivery of his/her micro-teaching session. Provide a few minutes for each person to share his/her feedback on one another's micro-teaching sessions regarding three strengths and three areas for improvement.

(Note 6)

Activity 3: *Asking good questions*

For self-study or a take-home task: Pick an article that students are required to read for discussion in one of your courses as the basis for practice in generating questions at different levels, using the following table.

For classroom instruction: Select a short article that is of common interest to all the participants. Have the students work in groups to help each other generate and develop a list of questions drawn from different levels of questions using the following table.

Levels	Your questions
Facts/Knowledge	
Comprehension	
Application	
Analysis	
Synthesis	
Evaluation	

6.5 Strategies for Success

A. Vocabulary strategies for maintaining fluency: Many international teaching assistants who speak English-as-an-additional-language share a perceived inability to use the monosemantic, specific words most frequently used by English speakers in a particular teaching or speaking context. While you continue to develop your ability to provide clear explanations, what you can do immediately is take responsibility for your own communication by making sure that you provide contextual cues that clarify your meaning. Here are ten vocabulary strategies from Smith, Meyers, and Burkhalter (1992) that you can apply in order to elicit help from your students when you cannot think of the exact word to use. Focus on getting your points across, and expand your communication toolkit by applying the strategies and language when you need them.

No.	Strategy		Example
1	**Parts**	Break the object down into *parts*.	I can't think of the word, but it has... [description of the object in parts].
2	**Cause and effect**	Describe what *causes* a phenomenon or what *results* from it.	I'm not sure what the word is, but it happens when....
3	**Comparison and contrast**	Talk about how the object is *similar* to or *different* from something else.	I don't know what it's called in English, but this object is similar to Y in [aspects], but is different from Y because it is....
4	**Definition**	Use a *definition* to describe what you mean.	The word I'm looking for means/can be defined as....
5	**Description**	Give the size, colour, shape, material, function, or other aspects of the object.	I can't find the word I am looking for. I'm talking about an object with....What's the word I'm looking for in English? I am not sure the correct word to use here. How would you describe....
6	**Example**	Give an *example* of what you are talking about.	The word just slipped my mind. What's the common way of describing...?
7	**Illustration**	Draw a *diagram* to describe the object.	Is there a word to describe something that looks like this?
8	**Nonverbal language**	Use your *body* or other visual means to demonstrate what you mean.	I am not sure how to say this, but it looks like this...
9	**Antonym**	Use its *opposite*.	I am not exactly sure of the word, but it's the opposite of....
10	**Synonym**	Use its *synonyms*.	I have the exact word at the tip of my tongue, and it's the same as....

(Note 7)

B. Ten pointers on teaching by discussion an article titled "Fine-tuning the craft of teaching by discussion" published by *Business Communication Quarterly*, I shared with its readers the top ten strategies for running discussions. If your TA responsibilities do not include running discussions, some of the strategies introduced in this article are still applicable in situations where you are chairing a discussion.

FINE-TUNING THE CRAFT OF TEACHINGBY DISCUSSION

EXTENSIVE RESEARCH IN cognitive psychology and education shows that discussion facilitates "depth of processing" (Craik & Lockhart,1972), which in turn promotes thinking, understanding, and retaining information. It is also well recognized that an effectively facilitated discussion is one of the most valuable vehicles for learning. In MBA classrooms, discussion is one of the most used instructional methods. As is also well known, the discussion process and outcome can vary in limitless ways, depending on the class objectives, the subject matter, the backgrounds of participants, the class dynamics, the facilitation style of the instructor, and the list goes on. Fine-tuning the skills involved in guiding classroom discussions is a valuable addition to an instructor's teaching repertoire, so that he or she may deal with both the expected and the unexpected.

This article presents the top 10 pointers derived from my own practice and from my instruction of future faculty (international teaching assistants), in my constant quest for ways to boost student learning and to elevate instructor skills at facilitating discussion. My experience has included both novice and experienced users of discussion methods across various contexts.

1. Expand Your Repertoire of Ways to Pose Questions

To a casual observer, discussion classes may appear to be disorderly and lacking in substance. A good discussion may unfold in unexpected ways, but the process and content are implemented with careful consideration and planning. The effective use of questions allows discussion leaders to channel students' thoughts, to direct and redirect interactions, to elicit important insights from participants, and to move the discussion along the logic of a teaching plan. The students benefit from taking in information and sharing it with others, as well as from the cognitive stimulation that the exchanges afford. In a plan for guiding questions, expand the questioning repertoire by using Bloom's(1956, 1984) taxonomy of thinking skills to help generate different levels of questions (*i.e.*, regarding facts, comprehension, application, analysis, synthesis, and evaluation).Vary questions to create opportunities for students to think at various levels of the taxonomy and to exercise critical thinking. Ask a wide array of questions at appropriate levels that move beyond the basics of who, what, when, where, and why. Try mixing informational questions with more abstract questions that will lead to the instructional objectives, such as asking students to describe and classify crucial elements in a case; to identify primary and secondary problems; to generate potential solutions; or to consider consequences, limitations, or the long-term impact of proposed solutions. As your questioning repertoire expands, your ability to deal with emerging questions and to quickly pose such questions at appropriate times in the discussion will also improve.

2. Begin the Discussion With a Familiar Experience and Keep It on Track

The dynamics of every session are different, and thus there are an infinite number of ways to start the discussion. For example, one may launch a discussion with a shared experience by referring to an excerpt from an assigned reading or to a public controversy, by asking for responses to assigned questions, by calling for anecdotes and experiences related to the topic, or by building on key points made in the previous session. No matter how you choose to begin a discussion, provide a sense of coherence as the class explores the ideas. Bring the discussion back to the topic if it starts to veer in other directions. One common student misperception about learning through discussion is that students learn less in discussions than in lectures. Provide summaries periodically and use the final 5 to 10 minutes to summarize progress made, linking the discussion to the objective(s) set forth at the beginning of the period, and pointing toward future classes or to the larger picture. It is important to stress the range of ideas rather than to imply that there is a "right" answer or solution.

3. Stretch Your Tolerance of Silence

The most common mistake made when posing questions in a discussions not allowing sufficient time for students to think and to answer the questions that are intended to stimulate and facilitate deep processing in students' thinking. Resist the urge to answer your own question. Your tolerance of silence after posing a question as well as after a response can enhance students' analytical and problem-solving skills. In situations where no thoughts or answers have been put forward, tyro continue probing by paraphrasing and rephrasing the question or by modifying the levels of questions that are within the students' "zone of proximal development" (Vygotsky, 1978, p. 86).

4. Exercise Effective Listening Skills

First, acknowledge contributions. Offer positive feedback, both verbally and nonverbally. Integrate participants' ideas, restate or paraphrase critical points, and offer encouraging comments to motivate learners' deeper engagement in the discussion. If a student makes an incorrect or inappropriate comment, put a positive twist on the comment and use the opportunity to explore the beliefs and assumptions that led to the comment.

Second, effective teaching by discussion demands the arts of suspending judgment and comment and of true listening and understanding. This calls for our alert involvement verbally and nonverbally and for observation of students' nonverbal language. Our preconceptions and experiences can limit our capacity to listen to and understand what is being said and what is meant. Listen for the verbal and nonverbal messages, for the content and assumptions expressed in the comments, such as underlying values, beliefs, attitudes, and assumptions. Seek every possible opportunity to help students build on each others' ideas. Stimulate students by your questions as well as theirs, and pursue the connections in the network of connected thoughts.

5. Facilitate Dialogue Among Participants and Foster an Inquiry-Driven Community

Foster a community of inquiry that supports learners' willingness to wonder, to pose questions, and to seek understanding through collaboration with others in imaginative handling of ideas and problem solving. Help students speak and respond to each other, not to you, through nonverbal language, such as maintaining eye contact with the entire group, and through verbal language, such as, "What do the rest of you think about Jack's comment that...?"As an alternative to the all-too-common practices of students arguing for and against positions, defending stances on issues, and providing information rather than asking questions, move the discussion from debate to dialogue. Help students to engage in "exploratory talk" (Barnes, 1992, p. 6) that provides a vehicle for coming to know—for developing the skills, knowledge, and dispositions needed for effective participation. This option is more instructive than mere reporting of what is already known. This, in turn, may generate broader thinking, newer insights, greater understanding, and more creative solutions.

6. Encourage Students to Explore a Variety of Viewpoints

As the instructor, solicit multiple interpretations and opinions and probe for differences before you weigh in with your own opinion. Play devil's advocate and encourage students to practice this technique as well. The purpose of challenging individual contributions, whether the challenges come from peers or the instructor, is to foster an imaginative, receptive mind; to make the contributor push his or her thinking further; and to help foster rigor in analyzing the subtler issues. Parker Palmer's assertion regarding good teaching can be extended to learning in a community in which the learner has "the courage to expose one's ignorance as well as insight, to invite contradiction as well as consent, to yield some control in order to empower [others], to evoke other people's lives as well as reveal one's own" (as cited in Barnes, Christensen, & Hansen, 1994, p. 6).

7. Help Students to Clarify Thoughts

Verbalized thoughts provide a basis for individual and group reflection. External speech serves as a mediating tool in the internalization of process and knowledge and in appropriation of conceptual content. Facilitating verbalization of unclear thoughts in a way that helps students explore their thinking offers opportunities for both instructor and students to challenge, discuss, and enhance cognitive processes. Clarifying thoughts through verbalization serves a strategic function in "other-regulation," where the instructor and other discussants provide the primary source of mediation, and "self-regulation," where the individual can resolve problems independently (Wertsch,1985, pp. 163-166). The clarification process is crucial to the ways knowledge changes among and within individuals during the co-construction process. Students' verbalization involves abstracting essential points from nonessential ones. This process is important for the development of mental actions and concepts and for the subsequent employment of such knowledge in solving a variety of problems.

8. Use the Linking Technique

This technique can be used throughout the various stages of discussion: to begin, to move, and to conclude a discussion. This may include linking the discussion to practical examples, to professional experiences, to analogies, as well as to comparisons and contrasts. Grasp opportunities to tie students' ideas and comments to other students' comments, to the topic, to other examples, to the bigger picture, and so on. Students should also be guided to ground their conceptual arguments in the details of their own personal, accumulated professional experiences, which have shaped their conceptual view of the case/issues under discussion. They should be encouraged to expand the sources of their personal theories-in-use.

9. Pay Attention to Individual Participation Styles

In addition to learning about participants' backgrounds in a way that will help you link their experiences to classroom discussions, vary your ways of eliciting participation by considering students' participation styles. For example, some individuals may find it challenging to speak up in a large group, regardless of the quality of their prior preparation. Cultural, social, and psychological factors may contribute to personal reluctance to speak in class. Encourage the "reluctant" or quiet participants to get involved by having all students write a response or hypothetical solutions to a case first and then work backwards to derive the analysis. Alternatively, use "warm" calls, for example, "Jack, would you be willing to offer your thoughts after Jane?" Warm calls provide advance notice to the reluctant participant, who may need more time to formulate thoughts. This method may prevent potentially damaging feelings of "losing face" and confidence. Also, using different discussion formats, such as lineup, mingling party, pyramid challenge, and poster tour, can enhance participants' involvement in class. Students can benefit from varied ways of participating, and this allows the instructor to achieve balance and broad participation.

10. Learn About Cross-Cultural Differences in Communication

It is useful for teachers to raise their awareness of the underlying cultural tendencies that can affect how people interact or participate in discussions. For example, it is useful to understand (without over generalizing or stereotyping) the relative emphasis on the individual versus the group, the tendency toward high or low context (Hall,1976), large versus small power distance, tolerance for ambiguity, attitudes toward conflict, and the impact of gender differences (Hofstede, 1997, n.d.).

In my years of teaching, I have found that students experienced the greatest number of "aha" moments about their own and other students' interaction patterns when they were introduced to the differences between high-and low-context styles, large and small power distance tolerance of ambiguity. Some common characteristics of high-context culture may include more emphasis on what is left unspoken(implicit and indirect), more reliance on nonverbal communication and shared knowledge/assumptions, more need for silence (longer inter-turn pauses), and preference for inductive rather than deductive processing patterns. In contrast, low-context communication tends to be direct, precise, and clear. Recognition of a wide power gap may lead to silence as a form of respect, rather than as a sign of being unengaged, as well as not taking initiative, not asking questions less willing to disagree or criticize authority, and being more accepting of the authority of written texts. People with strong uncertainty avoidance may exhibit a lack of tolerance for differing behaviours and opinions. They may be less flexible and have a stronger need for definitiveness and predictability.

Though interaction patterns may be deeply ingrained, it is important to keep in mind the interwoven and context-dependent nature of those cultural dimensions. As Barnes et al. (1994) pointed out, a successful discussion requires an effective partnership between the instructors and the students. Knowledge about our students strengthens the partnership, enables instructors to meet students where they are (which is where learning begins), and helps instructors to guide the discussion and their involvement in the process.

Conclusion

Listen to those who have achieved mastery or are persistent in practicing the art of teaching by discussion or to anyone who has been in enriching discussion classes. These instructors and learners will staunchly stand by their viewpoint that a well-led discussion can be one of the most rewarding and successful learning experiences for both students and teachers. Facilitating discussion is a difficult and demanding art of balancing structure and flexibility. Fine-tuning the craft of teaching through discussion takes time, practice, and patience. It requires the discussion leader's competence in managing both content and process (Barnes et al., 1994) to reach instructional/learning goals. Through ongoing feedback from colleagues and through self-reflection, mastery of the craft of teaching through discussion can be attained. Every discussion class provides an opportunity for intellectual adventure and new learning, and the rewards of exploring the territory of teaching through discussion are bountiful and ever-unfolding.

APPENDIX: Suggestions for Varying Discussion Teaching Formats(adapted from Dunne, 2004)

Suggestion 1: Lineup

1. Tape a line on the floor with, for example, "agree" and "disagree" on opposite ends.
2. Ask students to choose a place on the line according to your own position on the issue.
3. Share with those standing near them why you have selected the position. Provide examples, reasons, and explanations.

Suggestion 2: Mingling Party

1. Formulate a set of questions in advance.
2. Distribute the question sheet to each student before class to allow for preparation.
3. Ask students to circulate around the room and to share their research findings and thoughts on the questions.

Suggestion 3: Pyramid Challenge

1. Generate a list of questions that you want students to explore.
2. Ask students to work in pairs and discuss the assigned questions.
3. After the pair discussion, ask students to form a group of 3 or 4 to discuss the questions.
4. Re-gather the groups for a whole class discussion on the questions.

Suggestion 4: Poster Tour

1. Generate a list of no more than five key issues to be discussed.
2. Divide the class according to the number of issues and distribute a single flip chart sheet to each group.
3. Randomly assign issues to groups. Alternatively, let students self-select an issue that concerns them the most or is most relevant to their professional experience. Remind the students that each group should have approximately the same number of participants.
4. Ask each group to nominate a team facilitator and a record keeper.
5. Assign a time frame for students to complete the group task of generating ideas/solutions pertaining to the assigned issue.
6. Ask each group to put the issue at the top of the sheet and the answers in point form.
7. Pin the sheets to the wall around the classroom.
8. Request one member from each group to stay with its group's poster to answer questions from members of other groups.
9. Ask the class to circulate around the room in order to read other groups' posters.

C. Strategies for bridging the cultural/language gap in teaching: In the "Facing Challenges and Exploring Hidden Assumptions" section, you explored ways to bridge the cultural/language gap. Here are some strategies that you can apply when communicating with students.

1. Let your students know in your introduction how you'd like to be addressed. Repeat your name a few times because it may sound strange to your students. (For example: "My name is..., and it is pronounced as.... Please feel free to call me....")

2. Extend permission for assistance or interruptions. Don't apologize for your command of English; instead, let your students know that you are open to their help and corrections, and would appreciate their letting you know if something that you have said is unclear to them. (For example: "Sometimes I might have trouble finding the best words to express myself in English. If I hesitate, please feel free to pitch in." "If my pronunciation is off, if I have misspelled a word on the board, or if I am not being clear in my explanation, I hope you will let me know or ask me questions."

3. In your introduction, clarify your students' expectations early and upfront when you are providing course information. Don't expect your students to read the course outline; communicate the information in a low-context manner.

4. Be aware of your own tacit assumptions and expectations as well as those of your students. Listen and communicate empathetically. Being empathetic requires one to have a sense of self-awareness and knowledge about one's own feelings as well as the capacity to put oneself into someone else's shoes and understand what that person is feeling. This capacity is important, especially when another person's perceptions or ideas might be different from your own (Brown, 2006).

5. Practice, practice, practice. It is in the doing that we actually get better at communication.

UNIT 7

STEPPING OUT – CONFERENCE PRESENTATIONS, RESEARCH TALKS, TEACHING DEMONSTRATIONS, AND INTERVIEWS

7.1 Unit Introduction

Graduate students are attending and presenting at more conferences and are doing so at earlier stages of their graduate programs. The final unit introduces you to speaking situations at conferences, job talks, and interviews. This unit builds on the abilities to express opinions and respond to questions in interpersonal, group, and teaching settings that you have developed in previous units. These abilities are highly applicable to presenting at conferences, delivering research talks, giving teaching demonstrations, and speaking during job interviews. The recurring key components in this final unit, which include Facing Challenges and Exploring Hidden Assumptions, Mastering the Mechanics of Language, Application Activities, and Strategies for Success, are designed with the main focus on developing your confidence and competence in communicating with mixed, diverse, or unknown audience members in fielding challenging/unanticipated questions. The Application Activities provide opportunities for you to put all that you have learned in previous units into practice, with the aim of refining your ability to communicate your research according to the needs of your audience. The Strategies for Success section includes questions and tips for academic interviews and pointers about controlling speech anxiety.

The time is now to start preparing and practicing the delivery of the types of talks mentioned in this unit. Don't wait until your research is completed to present at conferences or until you have a firm call for an interview or a campus visit to start preparing what and how you intend to communicate in various scenarios and at various lengths – one-on-one meetings, group interviews, teaching demonstrations, and research talks. Finally, don't take rejections personally; treat every challenge as an opportunity for learning and for personal and professional growth!

7.2 Facing Challenges and Exploring Hidden Assumptions

Diagnostic questions: Explore these questions on your own if you use this book for self-study. In a classroom, share your thoughts about these questions with a speaking partner and be prepared to share your discussion with the class.

1. Share with your speaking partner(s) how you feel about your ability to answer questions during question-and-answer sessions at conferences or job talks. What challenges have you encountered or would you anticipate encountering? What cross-cultural factors might come into play in this context? Together, brainstorm strategies that you can use when fielding questions.

    Challenges:

    Strategies:

                                                                                                (Note 1)

2. Fielding Challenging Questions: Building on Unit 5, where you explored how you would handle seven types of questions that you might encounter during the question-and-answer sessions that occur in departmental presentations, explore with your speaking partner(s) some strategies that you can use to handle the following five challenging situations in the question-and-answer sessions that occur in conferences and job talks. Be sure to consider both the *strategies* (i.e., how would you deal with the situation?) and *language* (i.e., what would you say exactly?) that you can employ when handling each of the following situations. Work in pairs and make the effort to write down what you would say for each situation.

    Situation 8: A "don't know" question

    What would you do?

    What would you say?

    Situation 9: A hostile question

    What would you do?

    What would you say?

    Situation 10: A personal/confidential question

    What would you do?

    What would you say?

Situation 11: An "on a scale of one-to-ten" question

What would you do?

What would you say?

Situation 12: No questions!

What would you do?

What would you say?

Other: What are some other challenges identified in question 2? Together, brainstorm what you would do and say to help you overcome them.

7.3   Mastering the Mechanics of Language

(A) Functional language for delivering a teaching demonstration: Here are some useful
expressions that you can use in various parts of your talk for classroom teaching (Unit 6) or for delivering a teaching demonstration (or teaching demo) as part of a job talk. Modify or add any expressions of your own to suit your communicative purposes. The mechanics are introduced in this unit because you will have only one chance to deliver a teaching demo at each institution where you have been invited for an interview. As such, it's important that you plan and practice what you will say, not to only make your teaching of the content memorable and effective (e.g., by applying the strategies for enhancing clarity of explanations introduced in the previous unit), but also to create an impression of being polished and smooth in your linking and delivery of the important key points in various sections of your teaching session.

Section 1: The introduction of your lecture

To greet your class:

Good Morning! How's everyone today?

To warm up your class or make announcements:

I'll/Let's begin by taking a look at....
Are we ready to start?
First of all, let me remind you....
Before we move on to today's topic, let me make a few (important) announcements....
Before I introduce today's agenda, are there any questions related to what we covered last week?

To introduce the subject/topic:

Today's lecture will focus on....
Today, we are going to talk about....
This morning we are going to look at....
In this lab, I plan to cover....
Today, let's explore the answers to three questions that are often asked about....
As a continuation of what we talked about last week concerning X, the focus of today's lecture is on....
In the last class we examined.... Today we will spend the first half of the class on ... and then we will turn to....

To give instructions about questions:

If you have any questions, please feel free to stop me and ask me to repeat or clarify anything I say.

Try adding some of your own expressions:

_____

_____

_____

Section 2: The body of your lecture

To signal transitions between sections:

Next, let's move on to....
Turning now to....
Now, I'd like to shift our attention to....
(The first issue) leads us to the second issue about....
So far, we have discussed.... Next, I want to focus on....
So far, we have considered.... Now, I'd like to draw your attention to....

Now that we understand X, let us begin to consider Y.

Before moving on to the next category, let me give one more example.

Before going on to the next point, are there any questions?

Let's go on to the next aspect of....

So that explains the procedure, but what benefits does it have?

Using rhetorical questions as transitions: e.g., Where does this leave us? Where do we go from here? What can we expect from this?

To illustrate:

For example..../For instance....   In this case.... In another case....
Take the case of....   To demonstrate..../To illustrate....
As an illustration....   Let me give you an example to show....

To repeat or paraphrase:

That is...; in other words....   As I said/stated/described/mentioned earlier....
Let me put it another way/in a different way....   Let me repeat that again because the concept is very important....

To emphasize points:

The main thing is....   More important than this is....
Notice the differences between X and Y....   Let me say it again that....
The key point is...   It's important to emphasize, at this point, that....
This is the most crucial step in the process....   So that's a question that commonly appears on tests.

To check understanding:

Are there any questions so far?   Is everyone clear on the key components of...?
Is everyone still with me?   Is this clear to everyone?
A few of you look confused. Would you like me to explain that again?

To postpone questions:

That's a great question! You are slightly ahead of us. I'll be coming to your question in about five minutes. I will mention that to you when we get there.

Try adding some of your own expressions:

_____

_____

_____

Section 3: The conclusion of your lecture

To provide a note of finality:

Let me briefly summarize/recap what we have covered today. We've considered/examined the three points, that is (X, Y, and Z). Next week we will..../The question that I'd like you to think about is....

To invite questions:

Before I get to others' questions, let me try to answer the question X raised earlier.

Now, are there any questions?

Does anyone have any questions?

Are there any final questions?

To deal with questions after your lecture:

> I can't talk right now because I have to rush to a meeting, but I'd be glad to see you [day/date] after [time] or during my office hours.
> I'd be happy to discuss the assignment with you, but I have another appointment in 10 minutes. Why don't we schedule an appointment to do that?
> I have a scheduled event to attend right after this lecture, but I would be very happy to discuss your question after [time] today. Would the time be suitable for you?
> I have another talk to deliver across the campus. Would you like to walk with me? Then we can talk about your questions, if that arrangement works for you.

Try adding some of your own expressions:

_____

_____

(B) Communication strategies and language for fielding challenging questions:

1. A "don't know" question: Facing questions that you don't have answers for can be challenging to anyone, whether you are speaking English as an additional language, or whether you are a graduate student or an instructor. For speakers from large power-distance cultures, admitting that one does not know the answer can be even more difficult, because such an act counters one's belief about how teachers or presenters, who are "supposed to" be the subject-matter experts, should behave. The inability to deal with questions that you should have been able to answer and that were raised during departmental meetings, thesis defenses, conference talks, and so on is a problem that you should strive to avoid through preparation. When questions arise that you simply cannot answer or that require more research to address adequately, learn to say so! Try the following phrases, which will enable you to deal with such "don't know" questions in a professional manner.

- "I don't know the answer to your question, but I will find out and get back to you."

- In some situations, "redirecting" is a great strategy. For example, if you are teaching or are speaking to a group of people whose individual areas of expertise you are familiar with, or if there is someone in the audience whose expertise is known to you, you may try: "You know, I'm not really familiar with..., but, let me turn it over to the group: Does anyone have an answer to this question?" "You know, this is not my area of expertise, and I know that Dr. Weaver has done some work in that area. Dr. Weaver, would you like to comment on Dr. Huberman's question?"

- Use what I call the "AAA strategy" – Acknowledge, Admit, and Assume responsibility. For example: "That's a great question! (*Acknowledge*) I don't have an answer for you off the top of my head. (*Admit*) Let me find out and get back to you. (*Assume responsibility*)

2. A hostile question: You may have come across or witnessed (or will probably encounter) this kind of situation at a conference. Don't get discouraged if it happens to you. Learn the following strategies to address such a situation professionally and move on.

- Remain calm and address the question directly and factually. Some have found that including the questioner's name in public situations has the effect of toning the person down, because all of a sudden his/her name is known to all and the questioner has a reputation at stake.

- **Handling a question when you know the answer:** "Thanks for raising that question (and I appreciate your viewpoint.) I believe that [answer]. If you'd like to discuss this further, I will be glad to meet with you after the session and discuss it in more detail."

- **Handling a question when you don't know the answer:** "You've raised interesting points. I'd like to take the time to...."Postpone answering or redirect the question by following the strategies described in the "don't know" question situation.

3. A personal/confidential question: This may be a test of your discretion and professionalism. It is best to reply that you would prefer not to divulge any confidential information. Here are ways to handle questions that may be personal or confidential in nature and may not be relevant to your presentation.

> "That's a personal matter. Let's focus on issues related to the project...."
> "I am not at liberty to disclose that information due to ethics concerns."
> "I am not in a position to share that information because we are obligated to safeguard participants' anonymity."

4. An "on a scale of one-to-ten" question: For example: "On a scale of one to ten, how would you rate your...?" or "If you have to grade your X, what grade would it be?" Your "six" on a ten-point scale could mean something very different from another person's "six." Such numbers are highly subjective and relative. Instead of providing the questioner a number or a grade, provide concrete examples when answering this type of question.

- **On a matter that you feel quite confident about:** "Just giving you a number on X would be an oversimplification. I'd have to say instead that I have done... to enhance the trustworthiness of my research."

- **On a matter that you feel less satisfactory about:** "I agree that there is always room for improvement. However, I won't oversimplify the matter by just giving you a number. Instead, let me tell you what I have done/the steps I have taken to enhance.... First...."

5. No questions! We all remember those awkward moments when you could hear a pin drop after the presenter invites questions and comments from the audience. This silence could mean that you have done such a thorough job that there are simply no questions left, that your audience is completely lost and has tuned out, or that cultural factors may be at play in your audience's response or lack thereof!

- Carefully consider who your audience members are and their needs. In addition to making sure that you have done your homework thoroughly in getting ready for the talk, always prepare a few questions in advance. Sometimes your audience members just need some time to warm up during the question-and-answer session.

(Note 2)

7.4 Application Activities

Activity 1: *Research talks*(For classroom instruction or self-study)

When you are conversing formally or informally with professional or personal contacts at conferences or in the interview process, you will have various critical opportunities, some very brief and some lengthier, to describe your research to various kinds of audiences – fellow researchers in your field, researchers not directly in your field or outside of your field, potential future colleagues, students, and so on. It is crucial to be able to zoom in and out in your communication of complex ideas in a way that makes them accessible and interesting to the intended audience. This activity focuses on enhancing the clarity of language and context that is essential in conversing with people who have a wide range of areas of expertise.

Instructions: Present talks describing aspects of your research in four different ways.

1. Prepare to give a 10-minute talk aimed at a non-specialized audience. This is applicable to research talks or job talks that ask you to make your research accessible and interesting to faculty and students alike. Carefully consider the need to provide more context for the information and to not assume any background knowledge.
2. Prepare to give a 5-minute talk aimed at an audience with mixed levels of background knowledge. This is the scenario typically encountered when you speak at conferences and in all situations where time is a constraint. Consider what definitions need to be provided, what background information must be clarified, and what details should be eliminated.
3. Prepare to give a 3-minute talk aimed at a specialized audience. Be very precise and succinct in your description, without neglecting any essential definition or the background information needed for your listeners to understand the nature and significance of your research.
4. Prepare to give a 1-minute talk aimed at generalists. This is highly applicable to various formal and informal speaking settings. Focus on modifying your language and contextual information to make your talk accessible and concise, and to provide an account of the practical significance of your work. Ask yourself: What do you want your listeners to think about when they leave?

For classroom instruction: Instead of having students deliver all four talks at once, you may focus on one type per session/week. Ask students to take notes of each presenter's talk and, while doing so, to keep in mind such aspects as structure, content, clarity of context, clarity of language, nonverbal language, and vocal qualities (e.g., pace, volume, pitch, inflection, and pausing – refer to the Notes on the Units section for Unit 5, point 3). Set aside some time at the end of each session to allow participants to share their feedback and thoughts.

For self-study: Find people who are representative of three kinds of audiences and who are willing to offer feedback to you. If you cannot do that, try video-taping yourself practicing delivering three talks and critically evaluate areas for further improvement. Seek out feedback from others. Most universities have professional development or career centres that offer support for skill development.

Activity 2: *Mock academic interviews* (Take-home task)

Instructions:
1. Work in pairs to prepare and present a mock job interview.
2. Each student will take a turn being the interviewer and interviewee. Each interviewee will inform the interviewer about his/her target institution.
3. Use the questions in Section 8.5A to prepare both the questions and answers. The interviewer will select the appropriate questions to pose to the interviewee on the basis of his/her research about the target institution; the interviewee will anticipate the questions that the interviewer will raise.
4. The interviewee should write out and practice his/her response for each anticipated question.
5. When both are ready to present the mock interview orally, tape/video-record each interview session. The interviewer should take notes to (a) emulate what interviewers often do and (b) facilitate post-mock interview sharing and reflection.
6. Play back each of the two clips and reflect on each other's responses to various chosen questions in order to spot areas for improvement.

(Note 3)

Activity 3: *Learn from those who have walked the path* (Take-home task)

1. If you haven't had any experience presenting at conferences, informally interview three people that you know have had such an experience and ask them to share with you some "do's and don'ts" in their preparation and delivery of a conference talk. What have you learned?

2. If you are near the stage of an academic job search, informally interview three people whom you know have had experience giving job talks and ask them to share with you their experiences in delivering a research talk, giving a teaching demo, going through an interview with the search committee, meeting with faculty and students in the department, attending lunch/dinner functions, and so on. What have you learned from your conversations with them?

7.5 Strategies for Success

A. Preparing to answer questions in your academic job interviews:Here are some common possible question types and tips that I have accumulated from my experiences on both sides of the table: as a candidate searching for an academic position and as a member of a search committee selecting a potential colleague. Take time to go over them and prepare how you would respond to interview questions relevant to the position you are seeking.

Thesis:
- Tell us about your thesis. How did you become interested in the topic?

A few pointers:
1. Prepare your oral summary ahead of time. Have a short version (1 to 2 minutes) and a longer version (5 minutes or so) (in case more detail is requested). Also, have ready brief oral elaborations on, for example, methodology; major findings; theoretical background; empirical, theoretical, methodological, and practical implications; and the importance of your findings. Be precise, concise, interesting, and free of jargon.
2. Don't assume they've all read your writing samples. Display enthusiasm and confidence about your dissertation.
3. Remember that you know more than anyone else in the room about the topic.
4. Focus on the significance, contributions, and originality of your dissertation.
5. Be prepared to talk about how your dissertation relates to the work of others in the field, to your future work, and to the wider academic world or professional community in general.

Publications:
- How do you plan to revise you thesis for publication?
- What are some of your publications?
- Tell us about the papers that you are currently preparing for submission.

Research:
- Can you describe your research and what you are currently working on? What do you consider to be your most important research contributions?
- What is your research plan for this year/for the next two years/in the next five years? What are your plans for future research?(This is an assessment of the extent of your career planning and of your prospects for tenure. Be concrete in stating your short- and long-term goals.)
- What areas of research would you like to focus on if you are hired in our department?
- How do you see your research fitting into a department such as ours, where we have a number of areas of specialization? (Be sure that you do your homework and know the areas of specialization in the department to which you apply.)
- What have your greatest challenges been in your research, and how have you responded to those challenges? (For questions that invite you to reveal challenges and weaknesses, turn the questions into positive responses.)
- What are your ideas for supporting your research financially? Do you have any plans to apply for SSHRC/NSERC/NSF grants? If so, describe the project for which you are hoping to receive funding.
- What collaborations have you had in your research in the past? What is your style or manner of collaborating with others?

Teaching:
- Could you please describe your teaching experience?
- What is your teaching philosophy in general?
- Describe a course you would like to teach. Describe your approach to instruction and methods of evaluation.
- Which courses in our calendar would you be able to teach?
- How would you teach X course (e.g., psychology 101, research methodology course, etc.)? (Make sure your answer fits the needs of the university/department interviewing you.)
- What would be your approach to teaching a graduate course in X in terms of methodology and content? (Make sure your answer fits the needs of the university/department interviewing you.)
- How do you see the relation between your teaching and your research interests?

- What courses would you like to establish in our department at the undergraduate and graduate levels? How would you go about developing that area for students?
- Our students are asking us to offer a course on X. What would be your approach to responding to that call?
- How would your students describe you?
- In your teaching experience, what have your greatest challenges been and how have you responded to those challenges?

Service:
- Have you done any committee work? Which of our committees would be of most interest to you?
- What do you think the role of a thesis or dissertation supervisor should be?
- What kinds of experiences have you had supervising or advising graduate and/or undergraduate students on research projects?
- What kind of administrative or organizational roles have you taken on in the past? What do you think your strengths are in this area?
- What kinds of professional development or service activities have you been involved in?

Other possible questions:
- What attracts you to our institution?
- Why would you like to work at our university/department?
- What assets will you bring to our program?
- What qualifies you for this position?
- What are your major accomplishments?/What two or three accomplishments are you most proud of?
- What traits and/or qualifications do you have that make you well suited to this position?
- What would you like to tell us that's not on your CV?
- Are there any questions you would like to ask me/us?

Your questions: Always have a few questions ready from your background research of the institution, department, faculty, students, courses, ties with other departments, research foci, and so on. If your questions were answered during the interview, let the search committee know and be specific so that the committee knows that you have done your homework.
- Where do you see this department/university in five years?
- What's the teaching load like?
- What's the tenure process like?
- What is the institutional support for scholarly work (e.g., study leave, financial support for conference travel, professional development fund, teaching release)?

B. Tips for overcoming speech anxiety!" – Ah, yes, we all know that it's easier said than done! Here are
the top practical tips gathered from colleagues and students that you can apply to overcome potentially debilitating anxiety. Never expect any strategy to work smoothly and magically the first time you apply it. Experiment with different strategies at least a few times to find the routine that works the most effectively for you in overcoming speech anxiety.

1. **Do your homework.** Nothing is going to beat prior planning, preparation, and practice. Rehearse, rehearse, rehearse. The more familiar you are with your talk, the more confidence and less panic you will feel.

2. **Save yourself from unnecessary panicking.** Save yourself from having your mind go blank; **prepare supporting material** (visual aids, note cards, or scripts) to keep yourself from going blank or losing your composure. Always have a plan B for everything (e.g., saving multiple back-up copies of your slides), and, if any unforeseen disaster strikes, remain calm and proceed with Plan B, or seek help.

3. **Memorize the first 120 seconds**. Know the introduction like the back of your hand, so that you can start the presentation on a strong note feeling confident. When the opening is over, the butterflies will dissipate. Things usually get better as you go along.

4.   **Think positively and visualize your success.** See yourself as polished and professional. Remember that your audience wants you to succeed; no one is interested in spending time listening to a bad talk. Avoid black-and-white thinking that there are only two outcomes, i.e., complete success or complete failure.

5.   **Check out the location,** if possible (it's not always possible if the conference location is overseas, for example), and **arrive early.**

6.   **Dress professionally and comfortably,** so that you don't find yourself adjusting what you are wearing every two minutes.

7.   **Get your "gears" ready.** Before your talk, drink some water for dry mouth. If there is no water anywhere, try gently chewing your tongue to create saliva. Finally, exercise your mouth muscles, much like the warm-up you would do before a sports game or exercise.

8.   **Make the butterflies work for you.** Recognize that a modest amount of nervousness, the so-called "facilitative anxiety," can help you to convey your message with energy and enthusiasm.

9.   **Take a few deep breaths.** Try slowing down your heart rate by breathing in through the nose (expanding the diaphragm, with relaxed shoulders), holding your breath for five seconds (tightening your stomach muscle, fists and toes), and then exhaling through your mouth (releasing all tension). Repeat this at least a few times.

10.   **Gain experience. Experience builds confidence.** Listen to others present and pursue opportunities to speak or present. Practice where you can, when you can, and try to respond to what people say to you. Any practice is good - whether you speak to someone who is a native English speaker or not.

Do you have any other personal tips to share? Have you asked others about their tips? You might also consider asking other presenters whom you admire about their tips for overcoming speech anxiety.

NOTES ON THE UNITS

1. The speaking tasks that graduate students perform in various academic settings covered in this book (e.g., meeting with professors as a graduate student or a research assistant, presenting projects in class or at the department, engaging in or leading seminar discussions, teaching or meeting with students as a teaching assistant, presenting at professional conferences, and so on) are often inter-related. Fielding questions, for example, can occur in such contexts as course or departmental presentations, classroom teaching, conference presentations, and job talks. Asking questions may occur while participating in seminars or, in the teaching context, and during the process of leading a seminar or class discussion. I have introduced and focused on the mechanics and strategies that are most relevant to the specific settings focused on in the units, but I want to remind readers that each unit builds upon what was covered in the preceding units.

2. The challenges of adjusting to a new level of academic pursuit and life both in and outside of class at the graduate level can be daunting, even for those who speak English as their first language. The challenges faced by those who speak English as an additional language are compounded when the transition also involves multiple sets of personal, social, and cultural values, beliefs, and expectations, intertwined with linguistic barriers encountered in the various roles that they need to assume. The article "Getting the most out of the U.S. higher education experience: An inside perspective" by Edward Bodine of the University of California, Berkeley, centres on international students in U.S. higher education and the challenges that they face. Bodine's advice is applicable to international graduate students in the context of North America as a whole. His guidance is also consistent with the fundamental approach to reflecting on and examining one's cultural and educational expectations in various speaking contexts throughout this book.

Unit 1: Getting Started: A Guide to Key Terms and Concepts

1. An approach that has worked very well is to introduce concepts to students gradually as they arise or when they become particularly relevant in the various academic settings under exploration in each unit. Certain factors are pertinent to various settings; the recurring relevance and inter-relatedness of the various factors provide great opportunities for learners to revisit those factors, to explore how they come into play in particular settings, to integrate those concepts into their communication repertoires so that they can become aware of those important factors when they examine and reflect on their own choices regarding day-to-day speaking encounters. Suggestions for concepts or factors that instructors and learners may consider exploring or revisiting are offered in the notes for each unit.

2. Visit Hofstede's personal website for a definition of each of his cultural dimensions and a summary of his ideas about various dimensions of cultural differences: http://stuwww.uvt.nl/~csmeets/. On http://www.geert-hofstede.com/index.shtml, you can find information about Hofstede's dimensions for various selected countries. Although some have criticized Hofstede's research methodology, conceptualization of cultures, and high level of generalization (e.g., McSweeney, 2002), his work is undeniably influential and has generated extensive research across disciplines that validates his findings (see Søndergaard, 2002). Hofstede's research may still be open to further clarification, but his explanation of the dimensions helps learners to develop a mental framework, have a heightened awareness of the various dimensions that may help improve their own communication, and relate the dimensions and factors to their own experiences. It is essential to reiterate the importance of not over generalizing and oversimplifying

the complexity of human behaviour and human communication; doing so could lead one to judge another person's behaviour as representative of his/her culture or to adopt the view that people are mere products of some culture and can be defined simply by reference to the culture or country to which each individual belongs (Leki, personal communication, 2009).

Unit 2: Engaging in Interpersonal Communication

1. Suggested cultural factors to be discussed in this context: large/small power distance (e.g., in supervisor-student interactions), high/low context, and proxemics. Keep in mind the role that individual personality styles play in interpersonal conversations.

2. Writing emails to your instructors or supervising professors should always be done with care. You are strongly encouraged to refer to Swales and Feak (2004) for 10 useful suggestions for email communications, if you haven't yet had a chance to do so. Beverly Rachel's (2008) "You are what you e-mail," published in *Career World*, also offers useful tips and email "do's and don'ts" that are worth reviewing.

3. *Note to instructors:* You may choose to proceed to Part 1 in Activity 1: Telephone role-playing, under the Application Activities section on page 19.

4. *Note to instructors:* Before moving on to the mechanics for exiting conversations, you may choose to proceed to Activity 3: Conversational ball on page 20.

5. *Note to instructors:* After introducing students to the mechanics and strategies for entering, maintaining, and exiting conversations, give them a few opportunities to experiment: (a) apply what they have learned in class right after you have covered those components, (b) at the beginning of the next session, use the first 10 minutes for students to mingle again to review and apply what they have learned, or (c) encourage students to seek out opportunities to apply those linguistic and strategic tools in their everyday lives and to share their successes and challenges for support and feedback.

6. *Note to instructors:* Ask your students to provide their telephone numbers verbally without writing them down or to write a caller's telephone number while they are listening to it. I have noticed that the act of "translating" telephone numbers from the learner's source language to the target can be quite a challenge, even for advanced English-as-an-additional-language learners. You will probably notice three common scenarios: A student might (a) provide an incorrect number, (b) jot down an incorrect number or have trouble writing down what he/she has heard, or (c) state two different numbers if he/she repeats the number while leaving a telephone message. I have found that it's helpful to, first, ask students to repeat their own telephone numbers to the point that they can say them without consciously trying to match source and target digits. Second, share with students that they need to expand their tolerance of asking for repetition.

Unit 3: Participating in Group Settings I

1. Some of the top challenges that students have mentioned facing in group/seminar discussions include the following: shyness, lack of self-confidence, uneasiness about taking the initiative, lack of relevant knowledge of the subject/issue, the need to construct logically ordered arguments, being assessed academically, and persistent talkers' monopolization of time.

   Note to learners: Do you share some of those challenges? What is one thing that you can try in order to overcome the challenges that you have identified?

   Note to instructors: Encourage students to identify and share their personal challenges. This sharing serves three important functions: (a) it can clearly demonstrate that they are not alone in facing those challenges, (b) it leads nicely to having them work together to generate strategies that might help them overcome these common difficulties, and (c) it fosters a learner community of open sharing and support.

2. Suggested cultural factors to be examined in this context: individualism and collectivism, masculinity and femininity, and silence.

3. *Note to instructors:* Consider implementing this activity (and the informal debate in the next unit) a few times so that learners have an opportunity to increase their ability to participate and observe (both the amount and type of participation). Two pedagogical suggestions that have worked well in implementing this activity: (a) Consider having the observers use an observation form. The form with sample moves shown below can be modified to progress from fewer types of moves to a more elaborate set of moves to suit the application activities in Units 4 and 5. If necessary, clarify or review how one would define the following turns and come up with phrases or expressions for each type of turn. Then have each observer take notes on the type of participation engaged in by members of the group they have been assigned to observe. (b) Distribute the same observation form to all participants, but non-observer participants will keep track of their own participation. Using the form often will motivate participants to increase the amount and types of participation when they carry out the activities.

Move	Questioner Group	Expert Group
Initiate a question		
Offer a follow-up response of a factual statement		
Offer an opinion/comment in agreement		
Offer an opinion/comment in disagreement		
Offer an opinion/comment in partial agreement		
Ask a follow-up question*		
Summarize others' point(s)		
Acknowledge others' points		
Other		
Total number of turns		

* Note the types of questions covered Unit 4 (e.g., questions for clarification, elaboration, confirmation, and so on). If this activity is repeated after Unit 7, consider asking participants to observe the levels of questions raised (e.g., factual, comprehension, analytical, application, evaluative questions) using Bloom's taxonomy, which was introduced in Unit 7.

4. *Note to instructors:* Encourage students to use this list as a checklist for reflection after Activity 3 in the Application Activities section on page 33.

5. *Note to students:* You can use this list as a checklist for reflection after your participation in a group discussion. More pointers are provided in the second part of Participating in Group Settings (Unit 4).

Unit 4: Participating in Group Settings II

1. When discussing academic freedom and the way academic dialogues are exchanged, consider reading Deborah Tannen's (2000) article, "Agonism in the academy: Surviving higher learning's argument culture" published in *The Chronicle of Higher Education* (https://www9.georgetown.edu/faculty/tannend/pdfs/agonism_in_the_academy.pdf).

Note to learners: Read the first three paragraphs and reflect on your own experience in participating in seminar discussions. What are your observations about the ways academic dialogues are exchanged? What are some thoughts that arise from having read the rest of the article?

Note to instructors: This article can be used to generate discussion and exploration about academic conversations in small groups and in different settings and academic cultures that are the students' home environments. Encourage students to share their observations, experiences, and reflections about their participation in the home versus the target language culture.

2. Suggested cultural factors to be examined or revisited in this context: individualism and collectivism, large/small power distance.

3. *Activity 1:* Some of the major challenges shared by students include: adjusting to different food, adjusting to a different climate, being homesick, being a foreigner in a different culture, using a foreign language for study purposes, adapting to new styles of teaching and learning, thinking critically in a foreign language, organizing and using time efficiently, feeling uncertain about standards of work expected, participating in academic discussions, building relations with others in academic settings, academic writing, comprehending lectures and seminar discussions fully, and reading what is required and beyond in a timely manner.

4. *Activity 3:* Avoid assigning learners to represent one side of an issue right away. Provide some time for them to explore both sides and generate a list of five or more support points for each side before determining which side of the issue that each group will represent. Request each group to nominate or self-volunteer a team facilitator, who will elicit the opinions of those who might be reluctant to speak up; a speaker, who will be responsible for the opening statement; a summarizer, who will summarize the position and key points made by the group in the closing statement; and a time keeper and observer to make sure that the group's work is on track and to provide some feedback on the process of completing the task at the end of the activity. Allow for 20 minutes preparation time, 30 minutes debate time, and 10 minutes debriefing time, enabling participants to reflect on the process and the product of the information debate. (Refer to Note 3 in Unit 4 for suggestions on the form that both observers and participants can use to monitor participation.)

5. Not only is the topic on the advantages and disadvantages of international graduate students who speak English as an additional language in their roles as teaching assistants or research assistants of great interest and relevance to learners, but the activities provide valuable opportunities to critically examine both sides of the issue. In the case of an interview for a teaching assistantship or research assistantship position, students often have reported feeling more confident about addressing concerns that potential supervising professors might have, as well as about speaking confidently regarding their contributions to the position that they are seeking.

6. Use this list as a checklist for reflection after participating in a group discussion or informal debate.

7. Reese and Wells (2007) provide another activity that uses a card game to develop students' participation in seminars in graduate settings. Their article, which is freely available online through Sage Publications (http://sag.sagepub.com/cgi/content/abstract/38/4/546), describes the activity procedures and presents its rationale, benefits, and weaknesses. Instructors seeking to offer more practice opportunities for learners may consider implementing the activity.

Unit 5: Giving Departmental Presentations

1. Suggested cultural factors to be revisited in this context: high/low context and large/small power distance.

2. *Note to instructors:* Encourage students to brainstorm their challenges in dealing with question-and-answer sessions and write each question on the board before moving on to the next one. It's likely that you won't have sufficient time to cover all the challenges generated during the brainstorming session, and, as such, you might like to take a look at the challenging situations covered in Units 6 and 8 and then decide what questions to cover from the list of challenges generated by learners. At the end of the Facing Challenges and Exploring Hidden Assumptions sections (question 4 in Unit 6 and question 2 in Unit 8, specifically), students can write down the challenges that group members raised but

that were not included in the most commonly faced question-and-answer scenarios covered. This step is to make sure that all the challenges that students share will be addressed by the end of the two units.

3. Consider ways to enhance a speaker's vocal image by attending to the following seven key vocal elements of speaking. Various exercises readily available in theatre training can be used to refine one's vocal image in relation to these key vocal elements.

  - **Pitch:** A high pitched voice may lead one to be perceived as less credible and persuasive.
  - **Inflection:** The amount of fluctuation between the highest and lowest pitch. Avoid speaking in a monotone.
  - **Duration:** The longer a word, a phrase, or a syllable is stretched out, the greater the emphasis that is placed on it. For example: "I am reading my article" (spoken neutrally) vs. "I am reading *MY* article" (not someone else's), or, "I am *READING* my book" (i.e., not drafting).
  - **Pace:** The rate/pace of the speech could depend upon the urgency of the message, or on the speaker's nervousness or intensity. Embrace variety in pace.
  - **Volume:** You need to adjust the relative loudness or softness of your voice to the situation and the setting. If you speak too softly you may be perceived as timid, uncertain, lacking confidence, unsure about yourself, or lacking knowledge about your subject.
  - **Tone:** The emotion registered in the voice (e.g., warm and friendly, cold and authoritative) suggests your attitude. If your speech conveys interest and enthusiasm, your listeners will pay more attention to what you have to say. A smile on your face will put a smile in your voices, and this will often work even when you are not in an upbeat mood.
  - **Pause:** Using pauses effectively can (a) help you gather your thoughts, and (b) give the listener time to breath and to reflect on what you have just said. Also, the power of pause helps to signal transition, create impact, and draw audience members in. Studies show that you can pause for as long as four seconds in the middle of a sentence, and it will seem perfectly normal to listeners.

4. Here are some vocal, verbal, and nonverbal hurdles to consider:

  Vocal: e.g., using too many filler words (e.g., "em," "er," "ah," "like," "I mean," right," "you know") that clearly indicate to your listeners that you are thinking of what to say next; an overly nasal tone of voice; breathlessness; an upward pitch at the end of every sentence; mumbling; monotone (i.e., lack of inflection, emotion, and expression); clearing throat often; a strong accent that undermines intelligibility; being too loud or too quiet throughout the entire speech; speaking too fast (sloppy speech) or too slowly throughout the entire talk. Obtain feedback from others to see if you might be facing some of those issues. If necessary, voice training (e.g., Gates, 2000; Joseph, 1999; Lessac, 1997; Rodenburg, 1993; The Act of Teaching, Part 2: Physical and Vocal Exercises) may enhance your vocal image.

  Verbal: e.g., using slang; habitually using tag questions; overusing hedging statements; over-apologizing (this may be a culturally related preference); using words incorrectly; mispronouncing key words (take the time to practice how to pronounce them correctly); trailing off at the end of sentences (sounding less confident); rambling or being long-winded, having a disorganized and incoherent presentation.

  Nonverbal: e.g., constant pacing and/or swaying; staring at notes without making any eye contact with the audience; jingling coins or keys in pockets; constant tugging at an ear; assuming a posture that is slouching or too stiff; fidgeting; and lacking expression or having a negative facial expression. (Most nonverbal hurdles can be detected by reviewing one's presentation on video.) Although these behaviours may not have a detrimental impact, minimizing their occurrence will strengthen the nonverbal component of your talk.

5. In team or group presentation situations, decide in advance how to distribute the subjects or sections in the question-and-answer session (e.g., you may have people with varied areas of strength in charge of answering questions related to specific sections, such as literature, methodology, results, and so on). Most importantly, always support each other. Never publicly contradict or disagree with each other's remarks or explanations. Instead, build on each other's contributions using the language for contributing points that was introduced in Unit 5.

6. I often find examples from sources such as commercials, political debates, academic presentations, and great speeches (e.g., http://www.americanrhetoric.com/) to illustrate those points and to ask students to identify the speaker's rhetorical strategies. Finally, when students are asked to self-assess the recording of their own presentations

(Application Activity 2: Self-assessment), remind them to examine their own talk not just at the micro (e.g., grammar, mechanics, language use) and macro levels (e.g., organization, development, coherence). For students who become interested in learning more about rhetoric, refer them to Corbett and Connors (1999).

7. One of learners' most common misperceptions is that effective language use means using "sophisticated" words, phrases, or sentence constructions to convey their language ability, ideas and thoughts, or subject knowledge. When asked: "Should one speak to express or speak to impress?", almost all my students have said that "speaking to impress" is more important than "speaking to express." Instructors might consider discussing the importance of a learner's ability to communicate about his/her area of specialization or research; the learner needs to communicate his/her advanced knowledge to non-specialists in accessible, non-technical English. Communicating complex ideas in lay person's terms is often far more challenging than using verbal shortcuts, such as technical terms or jargon. Honing one's ability to communicate to express ideas and knowledge accessibly, precisely, and concisely to people of mixed backgrounds and knowledge levels is critically important in many contexts, including grant applications, presentations, or informal conversations with professional contacts.

Unit 6: Teaching in the Classroom

1. The Derek Bok Center at Harvard University produced an excellent video titled "Teaching in America: A Guide for International Faculty and What Students Want: Teaching from a Student's Perspective." The video presents a range of important issues related to, for example, facing cultural assumptions and barriers, dealing with language problems, preparing for class, and responding to students' concerns. Students have found it helpful to view the excerpts showing graduate teaching assistants across disciplines sharing their experiences and insights about communicating in the classroom. The Center also produces a series of excellent, highly recommended videos related to teaching and speaking in the classroom. Refer to the References and Further Reading list for the titles.

2. Suggested cultural factors to be examined or revisited in this context: tolerance of ambiguity, large/small power distance, high/low context, and gender roles.

3. *Note to instructors:* The situations presented in this question are designed to help students to explore linguistic and strategic tools that they can use to deal with teaching situations that they might find challenging. For learners who have some experience teaching in the classroom as teaching assistants, instructors may consider beginning this activity by asking about the challenging teaching situations that the participants have personally encountered before dealing with the 12 scenarios provided here.

4. You may choose to proceed to Activity 3: Asking good questions, under the Application Activities section on page 80.

5. To illustrate techniques for enhancing the clarity of explanations, I have used video clips from lectures, labs, seminars, and tutorials, which I have gathered from teaching assistants and professors and from YouTube. You could also have participants identify the technique(s) used if you choose to use video clips in this segment, before asking them to create their own examples of techniques they could use in their own teaching contexts. If time is a constraint, divide the class into eight groups. Have each group choose one technique and generate one or two examples of the technique to share with the class.

6. *Activity 2:* This activity can be used to prepare learners for teaching demonstrations, which are often required in the academic job interview situations covered in Unit 7.

7. *Note to instructors:* Prepare a list of words and have each student randomly draw one word from a box. Each student will self-select an appropriate strategy to use to practice maintaining fluency and eliciting listeners' help to come up with the word without telling them what it is. For a larger group, have students work in pairs or trios. Here are some words to get started: prejudice, atmosphere, rotation, gravity, pliers, flabbergasted, yam fries, a carcinogen, disinfectant, and a celestial body.

Unit 7: Stepping Out – Conference Presentations, Research Talks, Teaching Demonstrations, and Interviews

1. Suggested cultural factors to be revisited in this context: high/low context, large/small power distance.

2. In academic interview situations, there might be other types of challenging questions that are inappropriate or even illegal for interviewers to ask. Although the article published by *The Chronicle of Higher Education* is dated, the advice offered by Mary Morris Heiberger and Julian Miller Vick (2002) in their article titled "How to handle difficult interview questions" is still valid, because there is at least a chance that you will have to deal with one of the questions that others have faced.

3. This activity can also be used for classroom instruction, if time permits and the classroom atmosphere has developed into a supportive one. Have students do the preparation work involved in the task (e.g., researching institutions, preparing questions and answers, rehearsing) as an outside-of-classroom project. Then each pair of students can carry out a mock academic interview in class to elicit feedback. Alternatively, in addition to the one-on-one interview format, students can prepare at least two questions from each of the areas listed in Section 7.5A, and then simulate the interview format where one student needs to answer questions posed by a search committee. For the group interview format, have the students hand in their list of questions on the day of the scheduled mock academic interviews. Have five participants volunteer to play the roles of the search committee members and randomly select five questions to pose to the interviewee. Follow up on this activity by eliciting comments and suggestions from the instructor and participants.

REFERENCES AND FURTHER READING

The references in the list below refer to the sources used in each unit. In addition, carefully selected references and resources have been added as further reading for learners and instructors who are interested in learning more about various aspects of academic conversation skills.

General References for Teaching and Learning Academic Speaking Skills

Bodine, E. (n.d.). Getting the most out of the U.S. higher education experience: An inside perspective. Retrieved December 1, 2009, from http://krakow.usconsulate.gov/krakow/inside2.html

Feak, C. B., Reinhart, S. M., & Rohlck, T. (2009). *Academic interactions: Communicating on campus.* Ann Arbor: University of Michigan Press.

Folse, K. S. (2006). *The art of teaching speaking: Research and pedagogy for the ESL/EFL classroom.* Ann Arbor: University of Michigan Press.

Lazaraton, A. (2001). Teaching oral skills. In M. Celce-Murcia (Ed.), *Teaching English as a foreign language.* Boston: Heinle & Heinle.

Levine, R. D., & Adelman, M. B. (1993). *Beyond language: Cross cultural communication.* Englewood Cliffs, NJ: Prentice Hall.

McCarthy, M., & O'Keeffe, A. (2004). Research on the teaching of speaking. *Annual Review of Applied Linguistics, 24,* 26-43.

Reinhart, S. M., & Fisher, I. (2000). *Speaking and social interaction* (2nd ed.). Ann Arbor: University of Michigan Press.

Tarone, E. (2005). Speaking in a second language. In E. Hinkel (Ed.), *Handbook of research in second language teaching and learning.* Mahwah, NJ: Lawrence Erlbaum.

Unit 1: Getting Started: A Guide to Key Terms and Concepts

Buller, D. V. (1987/2005). Communication apprehension and reactions to proxemic violations. *Journal of Nonverbal Behavior, 11*(1), 13-25.

Freeman, J. (2003). The science of conversation: Training in dialogue for NNS in engineering. *IEEE Transactions on Professional Communication, 46*(3), 157-167.

Hall, E. T. (1976). *Beyond culture.* New York: Doubleday.

Hall, E. T. (1959/1981). *The silent language.* New York: Anchor Books.

Hall, E. T. (1966/1990). *The hidden dimension*, New York: Anchor Books.

Hall, E. T., & Hall, M. R. (1990). *Understanding cultural differences*. Yarmouth, ME: Intercultural Press. *Academic Communication Skills: Conversation Strategies for International Graduate Students*

Hofstede, G. (1997). Riding the waves: A rejoinder. *International Journal of Intercultural Relations, 21*, 287-290.

Hofstede, G. (2001). *Culture's consequences: comparing values, behaviors, institutions, and organizations across Nations* (2nd ed.). Thousand Oaks, CA: Sage.

Huang, L.-S. (2009/2010). The potential influence of L1 (Chinese) on L2 (English) communication. *English Language Teaching (ELT) Journal.64*(2). Oxford Journals, Oxford University Press. First published June 23, 2009, doi: 10.1093/elt/ccp03

Kim, M-S. (2002). *Non-Western perspectives on human communication: Implications for theory and practice*. Thousand Oaks, CA: Sage.

Kotthoff, H. & Spencer-Oatey, H. (Eds.). (2007). *Handbook of intercultural communication*. (Vol.7 of *Handbooks of Applied Linguistics*). Berlin: Mouton de Gruyter.

Lewis, R. D. (2006). *When cultures collide: Leading across cultures*. Boston: Nicholas Brealey Publishing.

Lustig, M. W., & Koester, J. (2006). *Intercultural competence: Interpersonal communication across cultures* (5th ed.). Boston: Pearson.

MacIntyre, P., Dornyei, Z., Clement, R., & Noels, K. (1998). Conceptualizing willingness to communicate in a L2: A situational model of L2 confidence and affiliation. *Modern Language Journal, 82*, 545-562.

MacIntyre, P., Baker, S., Clément, R., & Conrod, S. (2001). Willingness to communicate, social support, and language-learning orientations of immersion students. *Studies in Second Language Acquisition, 23*, 369-388.

McSweeney, B. (2002). Hofstede's model of national cultural differences and their consequences: A triumph of faith – a failure of analysis. *Human Relations, 55*(1), 89-118.

Mulhouse, V. H., Asante, M. K., & Nwosu, P. O. (2001). *Transcultural realities: Interdisciplinary perspectives on cross-cultural relations.* London: Sage.

Nakane, I. (2005). Negotiating silence and speech in the classroom. *Multilingua, 24*, 75-100.

Nakane, I. (2007). *Silence in intercultural communication: Perceptions and performance*. Amsterdam: John Benjamins.

Nelson, M. R., Brunel, F. F., Supphellen, M., & Manchanda, R. V. (2006). Effects of culture, gender, and moral obligations on responses to charity advertising across masculine and feminine cultures. *Journal of Consumer Psychology, 16*(1), 45-56.

Saville-Troike, M. (1985). The place of silence in an integrated theory of communication. In D. Tannen & M. Saville-Troike (Eds.), *Perspectives on silence* (pp. 139-162). Norwood, NJ: Ablex.

Scollon, R., & Scollon, S. W. (2001). *Intercultural communication: A discourse approach* (2nd ed.). Boston: Blackwell.

Søndergaard, M. (2002). "In my opinion" - Mikael Søndergaard on "cultural differences." Retrieved November 5, 2009, from http://geert-hofstede.international-business-center.com/Sondergaard.shtml

Spencer-Oatey, H. (Ed.). (2000/2008). *Culturally speaking: Managing rapport through talk across cultures*. London: Continuum.

Tannen, D. (1990). *You just don't understand: Women and men in conversation.* New York: Ballantine.

Tannen, D. (1996). Researching gender-related patterns in classroom discourse. *TESOL Quarterly30(2)*: 341-344. Retrieved December 1, 2009, from https://www9.georgetown.edu/faculty/tannend/pdfs/researching_gender-related_patterns_in_classrom_discourse.pdf

Ulijn, J. M., & Campbell, C. (1999). Technical innovations in communication: How to relate technology to business by a culturally reliable human interface. In T. Malkinson (Ed.), *IEEE Professional communication conference record* (pp. 109-120). New Orleans.

Ulijn, J. M., & Kumar, R. (1999). Technical communication in a multicultural world: How to make it an asset in managing international business. Lessons from Europe and Asia for the 21st century. In P. J. Hager & H. J. Schriber (Eds.), *Managing global discourse: Essays on international, scientific and technical communication* (pp. 319-348). New York: Wiley.

Wood, J. (2001). *Gendered lives: Communication, gender, and culture* (4th ed.). Belmont, CA: Wadsworth.

Unit 2: Engaging in Interpersonal Communication

Chambers, H. E. (2001). *Effective communication skills: For scientific and technical professionals.* Cambridge, MA: Perseus Publishing.

Marton, B. A., et al. (2004). *Face-to-face communications for clarity and impact.* Boston: Harvard Business School Press.

Nichols, R. G., & Stevens, L. A. (1999). Listening to people. *Harvard Business Review on Effective Communication.* Boston: Harvard Business School Press.

Swales, J. M., & Feak, C. B. (2004) *Academic writing for graduate students: Essential tasks and skills* (2nd ed.). Ann Arbor: University of Michigan Press.

Tannen, D. (1995). The power of talk: Who gets heard and why. *Harvard Business Review* 73. Retrieved December 1, 2009, from https://www9.georgetown.edu/faculty/tannend/pdfs/the_power_of_talk.pdf

Unit 3: Participating in Group Settings I

Aristotle. 1954. *Rhetoric* (W. R. Roberts, Trans.). New York: Random House.

Corbett, E. P. J., & R. J. Connors. 1999. *Classical rhetoric for modern student* (4thed.). Oxford: Oxford University Press.

Green, C. F., Christopher, E. R., & Lam, J. (1997). Developing discussion skills in the ESL classroom. *ELT Journal, 51*(2), 135-143.

Jordan, R. R. 1997. *English for academic purposes: A guide and resource book for teachers.* Cambridge: Cambridge University Press.

Lam, W., & Wong, J. (2000). The effects of strategy training on developing discussion skills in an ESL classroom. *ELT Journal, 54*(3), 245-255.

Madden, C. G., & Rohlck T. N. (1997). *Discussion and interaction in the academic community.* Ann Arbor: University of Michigan Press.

Reese, C., & Wells, T. (2007). Teaching academic discussion skills with a card game. *Simulation Gaming, 38*(4), 546-555.

Sather, T., Ed. (1999). *Pros and cons: A debater's handbook* (18th ed.). London: Routledge.

Tannen, D. (2000, March 31). Agonism in the academy: Surviving higher learning's argument culture. *The Chronicle of Higher Education, 46*(30), B7-8.

Zhu, W., & J. Flaitz. (2005). *Using focus group methodology to understand international students' academic language needs: A comparison of perspectives.TESL-EJ, 8* (4).Retrieved December 30, 2009, fromhttp://www.tesl-ej.org/wordpress/past-issues/volume8/ej32/ej32a3/.

Unit 4: Participating in Group Settings II

Huckin, T. N., & Olsen, L. A. (1991). *Technical writing and professional communication for nonnative speakers of English* (2nd ed.). Boston: McGraw-Hill.

Leki, I. (2001). A narrow thinking system: Nonnative-English speaking students in group projects across the curriculum. *TESOL Quarterly, 35*(1), 39-66.

Nakane, I. (2007). *Silence in intercultural communication: Perceptions and performance.* John Benjamins.

Sather, T. (1999). (Ed.). *Pros and cons: A debater's handbook.* (18th ed.). London: Routledge.

Tatar, S. (2005). Classroom participation by international students: The case of Turkish graduate students. *Journal of Studies in International Education, 9*, 337-355.

Tennen, D. (2000). Don't Just Sit There–Interrupt!' Pacing and Pausing in Conversational Style. *American Speech* 75.4 (2000): 393-395. (https://www9.georgetown.edu/faculty/tannend/pdfs/Don't_Just_Sit_There-_Interrupt.pdf)

Williams, J. M., & Colomb, G. G. (2003). *The craft of argument: Concise edition.* New York, NY: Longman.

Unit 5: Giving Departmental Presentations

Alley, M. (2003). *The craft of scientific presentations: Critical steps to succeed and critical errors to avoid.* New York: Springer Science+Business Media, Inc.

Bourne P. E. (2007). Ten simple rules for making good oral presentations. *PLoS Computational Biology, 3*(4): e77. doi:10.1371/journal.pcbi.0030077

Carpenter, R. H. (1999). *Choosing powerful words: Eloquence that works.* Boston: Allyn and Bacon.

Fowler, L. (2000). Giving good technical presentations. *IEEE Instrumentation and Measurement Magazine, 3*(1): 35-38.

Gates, L. (2000). *Voice for performance.* New York: Applause Books.

Greenbaum, S., & Whitcut, J. (1987). *The complete plain words* (3rd ed.). London: Penguin.

Henninger-Chiang, T., & Reel J. (2001). *Professional presentations: How to succeed in international business.* Ann Arbor: University of Michigan Press.

Holliday, M (2000). *Secrets of power presentations* (2nd ed.). Franklin Lakes, NJ: Career Press.

Hughes, D., & Phillips, B. *The Oxford Union guide to successful public speaking.* London: Virgin Publishing Ltd.

Joseph, A. S. (1999). *Vocal awareness: how to discover, nurture, and project your natural voice.* Sounds True Video.

Kearney, P & Plax, T. G. (1996). *Public speaking in a diverse society.* London: Mayfield Publishing Company.

Lessac, A. (1997). *The use and training of the human voice: A bio-dynamic approach to vocal life* (3rd ed.). Mountain Views, CA: Mayfield Publishing Company.

Li, V. O. K. (1999). Hints on writing technical papers and making presentations. *IEEE Transactions on Education, 42*(2): 134-137.

McKerrow, R. E., Gronbeck, B. E., Ehninger, D., & Monroe, A. H. (2003). *Principles and types of public speaking.* (15th ed.). Boston: Allyn and Bacon.

National Institutes of Health plain language training program: http://plainlanguage.nih.gov/CBTs/PlainLanguage/login.asp

Novis, M. (2004). *Canadian public speaking.* Toronto, ON: Pearson Education Canada Inc.

Rodenburg, P. (1993). *The need for words: Voice and the text.* New York: Routledge.

Tufte, E. R. (2001). *The visual display of quantitative information.* Cheshire, CT: Graphics Press.

Walters, D. E., & Walters, G. C. (2010). *Scientists must speak* (2nd ed.). London: Routledge

Zarefsky, D. (2002). *Public speaking: Strategies for success.* Boston, MA: Allyn and Bacon.

Unit 6: Teaching in the Classroom

Barnes, D. (1992). *From communication to curriculum.* Harmondsworth, UK: Penguin.

Barnes, L. B., Christensen, C. R., &Hansen, A. J. (1994). *Teaching and the case method: Text, cases, and readings* (3rd ed.). Boston: Harvard Business School Press.

Bloom, B. S. (Ed.). (1956). *Taxonomy of educational objectives: The classification of educational goals (Handbook 1: Cognitive Domain).* New York: McKay.

Bloom, B. S. (1984). *Bloom taxonomy of education objectives.* Boston: Allyn & Bacon.

Christensen, C. (2007). The art of discussion leading: A class with Chris Christensen and the art of the lecture: Justice, a Harvard University Course in Moral Reasoning, The Derek Bok Center Series On College Teaching.

Craik, F. I. M., & Lockhart, R. S. (1972). Levels of processing: A framework for memory research. *Journal of Verbal Learning and Verbal Behaviour, 11,* 671-684.

Dunne, D. (2004). *Discussion teaching techniques.* Faculty Development Workshop Series. Toronto: University of Toronto.

Gorsuch, G., Meyers, C. M., Pickering, L., & Griffee, D. T. (2010). *English communication for international teaching assistants.* Long Grove, IL: Waveland Press, Inc.

Hall, E. T. (1976). *Beyond culture.* New York: Doubleday.

Hofstede, G. (1997). *Cultures and organizations: Software of the mind* (2nd ed.). London: McGraw-Hill.

Manser, M. H. (Ed.). (2003). *Good word guide: Answers everyday language problems.* London: Bloomsbury.

Mckeachie, W. J. (2002). *McKeachie's teaching tips: Strategies, research, theory for college and university teachers.* Boston: Houghton Mifflin Company.

Morgan, N., et al. (2004). *Presentations that persuade and motivate.* Boston: Harvard Business School Press.

Ross, C., & Dunphy, J. (Eds.). *Strategies for teaching assistant and international teaching assistant development: Beyond micro teaching.* San Francisco, CA: Jossey-Bass

Smith, J., Meyers, C. M., Burkhalter, A. J. (1992). *Communicate: Strategies for international teaching assistants.* Regents/Prentice Hall.

Tennan, D. (2001). Teachers' classroom strategies should recognize that men and women use language differently. In McPhee, J. & C. Rigolot (Eds.). *The Princeton anthology of writing: Favorite pieces by the Ferris/McGraw writers at Princeton,* Princeton, NJ: Princeton University Press.

Tobin, K., & Fraser, B. J. (1990). What does it mean to be an exemplary science teacher? *Journal of Research in Science Teaching, 27*(1), 3-25.

van Rooyen, H. G. (1994). The quest for optimum clarity of presentation: Context creation as teaching skill. *The American Biology Teacher, 56*(3), 146-150.

The act of teaching part 1: Theater techniques for classrooms and presentations. The Derek Bok Center Series on College Teaching. Boston: Harvard University.

The act of teaching part 2: Physical and vocal exercises. The Derek Bok Center Series on College Teaching. Boston: Harvard University.

Teaching in America: A guide for international faculty and what students want: Teaching from a student's perspective, The Derek Bok Center Series on College Teaching. Boston: Harvard University.

How to speak: Lecture tips from Patrick Winston. Technically speaking: Making complex matters simple. The Derek Bok Center Series on College Teaching. Boston: Harvard University.

Unit 7: Stepping Out – Conference Presentations, Research Talks, Teaching Demonstrations, and Interviews

Chronicle of Higher Education: http://chronicle.com/article/The-Academic-Job-Interview-/44607/ (The Advice section in The Chronicle of Higher Education contains a wealth of advice that is worth bookmarking.)

Heiberger, M. M., & Vick, J. M. (1998). What to do when they say, 'Tell us about your research.' *Chronicle of Higher Education.* Retrieved December 30, 2009, from http://chronicle.com/article/What-to-Do-When-They-Say-/46433/

Cottingham, K. L. (n.d.). Questions to ask (and be prepared to answer) during an academic interview. Retrieved December 1, 2009, from http://www.dartmouth.edu/~gradstdy/careers/services/interview/acad.html

Daly, J. and Engleberg, I. (1999, June). Coping with stagefright: how to turn terror into dynamic speaking. *Harvard Management Communication Letter.*

Desberg, P. (1996). *No more butterflies: Overcoming stagefright, shyness, interview anxiety, and fear of public speaking.* Oakland, CA: New Harbinger.

Golde, C. M. (1999). "After the offer, before the deal: Negotiating a first academic job." *Academe, 85*(1), 44-49.

Heiberger, M. M., & Vick, J. M. (1999). How to handle difficult interview questions. *The Chronicle of Higher Education.* Retrieved December 30, 2009 from http://chronicle.com/article/How-To-Handle-Difficult-Int/45704/. (Although the article is dated, the advice offered by Heiberger and Vick is still valid).

Heiberger, M. M., & Vick, J. M. (2002). *The academic job search handbook* (3rd ed.). Scholarly Book Services Inc.

Kling, J. (1999). Talking science with nonscientists: A personal communication, *Scientist, 13*(7), 12.

Kronenfeld, J. J., & Whicker, M. L. (1997). *Getting an academic job.* Thousand Oaks, CA: Sage Publications.

Linte, C. A. (2008). The art of dissemination: What makes an effective scientific presentation?*IEEE Engineering in Medicine and Biology Magazine. 27*(4), 5-8.

Linte, C. A. (2009). Communicating your research in lay language.*IEEE Engineering in Medicine and Biology Magazine. 28*(3), 5-7.

Modern Language Association: Interviews, Campus Visits, Job Talks, and Teaching Demonstration: http://www.mla.org/job_interviews

Stanford University I-Rite/I-Speak: http://www.stanford.edu/group/i-rite/about.html

Academic Job Interviews:http://serc.carleton.edu/NAGTWorkshops/careerprep/jobsearch/interviewing.html

SUBJECT INDEX

ABOUT THE AUTHOR

Li-Shih Huang is Assistant Professor of Applied Linguistics and Learning and Teaching Scholar at the University of Victoria. She completed her Ph.D. at the Ontario Institute for Studies in Education of the University of Toronto (OISE/UT). Prior to joining the University of Victoria, she taught at the University of Toronto.

Li-Shih has over a decade of instructional and curriculum design experience in EAP, ESP, ESL, and EFL at the university and graduate levels. Her creativity in designing pedagogical materials has been recognized by the international professional association TESOL, which awarded her the Mary Finocchiaro Award for Excellence in the Development of Pedagogical Materials.

Li-Shih's teaching and research interests include applied linguistics, second language acquisition, English for academic purposes across disciplines, and language learning and use strategies. Her current research projects include: academic communication needs and outcomes assessment across disciplines; the acquisition and usage of grammatical knowledge using a corpus-aided discovery learning approach; and modalities of reflection on second language learners' strategy use and oral production.

Website: http://web.uvic.ca/ling/faculty/huang.htm

9 780761 852803